STRANGER

Peter A Stankovic

Publisher: Sydney School of Arts & Humanities
15-17 Argyle Place Millers Point NSW 2000
www.ssoa.com.au
Stranger
ISBN: 9780995421981 print book
        9780995421974 ebook

Cover design by Ferdinando Manzo. Text design by Ferdinando Manzo. Typeset in Times New Roman. Printed and bound by Lightning Source as a POD paperback.

National Library of Australia Cataloguing-in-Publication data:
Stankovic, Peter author.
Stranger/ Peter Stankovic.
ISBN: 9780995421981
Fiction – crime fiction – Sydney novel – Australian fiction

Dedication

For my wife Glenda and my sons,
Alexander, Michael and Harry

Acknowledgements

I would like to thank Christine Williams and members of her Friday Writer's Group who listened to parts of my novel and provided useful feedback. I would also like to thank Lisa Creffield and Suganthi Singarayar for reading the novel and giving comments. Finally my thanks to the editor, Sharon Dean, for providing valuable editing services, and Ferdinando Manzo for cover design and text formatting.

Author biography

Peter Stankovic started his career as a chartered accountant and over the years became an independent finance professional. Writing was something he did occasionally until he retired from his finance career. He then took up full time writing and has published three other works. He lives with his family in Sydney, Australia. Other novels by Peter Stankovic are: LACK OF AMBITION, CHEATERS and CROOKS AND LOSERS.

Contents

Chapter 1: Sunday   11

Chapter 2 Sunday   17

Chapter 3 Sunday   22

Chapter 4 Sunday/Monday   26

Chapter 5 Monday   32

Chapter 6 Monday   38

Chapter 7 Tuesday   42

Chapter 8 Tuesday   47

Chapter 9 Wednesday   50

Chapter 10 Thursday   56

Chapter 11 Thursday   60

Chapter 12 Thursday/Friday   66

Chapter 13 Saturday   72

Chapter 14 Saturday   77

Chapter 15 Sunday   83

Chapter 16 Monday   88

Chapter 17 Monday   93

Chapter 18 Tuesday   97

Chapter 19 Tuesday   103

Chapter 20 Wednesday   106

Chapter 21 Wednesday   110

Chapter 22: Thursday   116

Chapter 23 Friday   122

Chapter 24 Friday/Saturday   129

Chapter 25 Saturday   134

Chapter 26 Saturday   138

Chapter 27 Sunday   141

Chapter 28 Sunday   146

Chapter 29 Monday   150

Chapter 30 Tuesday   156

Chapter 31 Wednesday   161

Chapter 32 Thursday   166

Chapter 33 Thursday/Friday   170

Chapter 34 Friday   176

Chapter 35 Friday/Saturday   184

Chapter 36 Saturday   189

Chapter 37 Saturday/Sunday   194

Chapter 38 Monday   200

Chapter 39 Tuesday   209

Chapter 40 Saturday   215

Chapter 41 Sunday, several weeks later 220

Chapter 1: Sunday

My eyes squint half open as I wake – my dream of exploding stars fades. A noise somewhere. But what is it? A door shutting? An object dropping? I open my eyes fully. I have a headache. Probably a hangover I imagine. I'm in a strange room. Painted apricot and white, the walls are too bright for this early in the morning, assuming it is morning. I'm also in a strange bed. The bed is large – queen sized, I guess – and somebody had occupied the space beside me, judging from the blanket partially pushed aside.

I hear activity outside. Who's there? Is it my sleeping companion? I sit up and rub my face. My head is splitting. I need water. I can't recall how I managed to get to this strange place and it worries me. What if I've been kidnapped? Tortured? No, I don't feel any pain. Or more to the point with the right side of the bed slept in, was I forced to make love to a woman? Against my will? Was she demanding or ugly or simply horrible? Surely I'd remember.

I shuffle out of bed and notice I'm naked. I search for something to wear. I find a man's jockey underdaks on a chair piled high with clothes, some male and some female. Trusting the underwear is mine, I pull on the underpants and walk to the door, listening for anybody immediately outside. I'm not yet in the mood to meet people and utter polite words. As I'm regarding my situation I see that the room has a dressing table with an oval mirror and cosmetics sorted neatly so I assume it's a woman's bedroom. Did I have sex willingly? I can't even remember that. Did I go drinking? Who would know?

The bathroom is opposite the bedroom, across a hallway, and

thankfully it's empty. After ensuring that nobody is around I pad over soft cream carpet to the bathroom. I close the door and wander over to the basin and look in the mirror. Who is this staring back at me? I come to realise after an awful second that it's me although I seem to have forgotten how I look. I'm Caucasian, from the initial inspection, with a slightly olive toning and I possess straight dark hair. I rub my chin, figuring the dark stubble over it is about a day or two old. There seems to be a bit of a bruise on my cheek. I wonder if I've been in a fight but dismiss the idea, as I can't recall any altercation. The surface of my face, as I examine it more thoroughly, is rough to the touch. I'm trim, not tall nor short and I seem to have good muscle definition, which suggests I work out regularly – but again, I can't recall what I do. This hangover is really bad.

I can't find an unused toothbrush so I squeeze some Colgate toothpaste onto my finger and rub it across my teeth and gums. I rinse with tap water. To my right is a shower stall. I climb inside and turn on the hot water tap. At first cold water gushes out. As the water flows over me I wonder whether my lack of memory is temporary because of a heavy session with alcohol. What's odd is that I can't even recall my name. I should be concerned but there's no point in worrying at the moment. All in good time. Besides, something might jog my memory. I succeed in completing a warm shower and it wakes me up a little more. Using the first towel I see, probably belonging to the female I suspect lives here, I dry off, put the underdaks back on and move out of the bathroom. Back in the bedroom, I dress and stretch as I consider my next move. I open the door again, hesitantly, and finally walk down the hall into a kitchen.

At first I can't see anybody. I look around. The kitchen is brightly lit by numerous round recessed ceiling lights although it's eight o'clock in the morning. It's overcast outside but not dark enough to justify interior lights being on. But who am I to complain? It's not my electricity bill. Coffee is brewing and the stove has a pan with something frying in it. Then as a storage cupboard door closes, I see a woman. She is imposing, with muscular bare legs and a strong looking torso. Big breasts. A nice curvy figure. Who is she?

When she sees me she smiles. 'Hello there. Finally awake?' she says pleasantly.

'Yes,' I say. But I don't know what else to say. Do I say I can't remember last night? Do I say I don't remember her? Do I ask what happened? It seems so lame. Perhaps it's best to keep my cards close to my chest right now. See what transpires.

'Hungry?'

'Ravenous,' I say. 'Can I help with something?'

'No, you sit down and I'll be with you with breakfast in a moment,' she says. The slight English accent makes each word sound precise. Sharp. Clear. Lovely.

I have no recollection of her name so it's awkward to say too much. 'Thanks,' I mutter, not sure whether I should stay or go.

So the rather attractive curvy woman comes over and serves me bacon, eggs, baked beans and tomato with toast and coffee. It looks fantastic and I almost feel embarrassed, being so useless, but I simply eat, not saying anything.

'How did you sleep?' she asks.

I look at her. She has beautiful penetrating hazel eyes. 'Good. And you?'

'You don't remember, do you?'

'I have a headache.'

'Of course you do. You can certainly put away the liquor. Boy oh boy. Stay there. I'll get you some Panadol.'

She leaves and returns a moment later with two tablets and a glass of water. 'Here,' she says, 'So you don't remember much about last night?'

I swallow the Panadol with water and place the glass on the table. She sits down across from me and continues with her breakfast, awaiting my response. 'Not much. Well, nothing if truth be told.' I have to own up. No use in pretending I know when I haven't the foggiest

13

about anything.

'Last night a group of my friends were celebrating at The Anchor for my twenty-ninth birthday.'

'Where's that?'

'Campbell Parade just as you round Bondi Road. Inside it has dark timber, a small bar and a handful of tables. Remember?'

'Not really,' I say because I have no clue.

'Never mind. I was with six others. Three couples and me. Pretty sad, actually. At some stage you joined us and I think you'd already had a few drinks. But you were funny, giving us some witty insights about being stranded and stood up and we had no idea what you were on about. We carried on and the group let you join in our celebration. We all had burgers and beer and wine.'

'Ok.' I finish the plate of bacon, eggs and extras. It was delicious and, should I win this girl over, I hope she will continue to cook for me.

'Well around midnight a man, probably drunk, followed you from the bar and punched you and you fell and hit your head on a wooden bench.'

'Who was he?'

'No idea but Rodney, Max and John pushed him out of the pub and told him to get lost. You got up but and carried on as if nothing happened except that you seemed out of it. So we just continued on partying.'

'I see,' I say.

'When I suggested sharing a taxi you agreed. Then at my place you didn't know where you lived. So, thinking that you were suffering from too much drink, I suggested you come in to recover and here you are.'

'Very kind of you. Didn't the others worry about you taking a strange man home?'

'They left while I was in the restroom. I couldn't leave you there as you seemed totally disoriented.'

14

'Nice friends,' I say.

'Perhaps they wanted to give us some quiet time as we seemed to be enjoying a chat about … I can't recall now myself.'

I don't know what to say. 'Thanks,' I manage, but I'm sure this isn't good enough. 'How can I repay you?'

'First you probably need to see a doc, if you still can't remember anything from last night.'

'Right. Well I can't recall anything at all.'

'My God, you'll have to go to the hospital straight away.'

I want to understand who I am first. I'll check my wallet, if I can find it. 'Let's not panic. I'll do that if necessary but I suspect my memory will return in due course. Besides, I hate doctors.'

She laughs. 'How do you know? You can't remember, remember?'

'No idea. Probably instinct. So tell me, what happened … ' She's probably right in suggesting I go visit a hospital but something holds me back. Did I have a bad experience?

'You're wondering whether we had sex,' she says.

'Well, yes … I don't even know your name.'

She smiles and her whole face lights up. 'I'm Jackie. And we didn't do it. You passed out after I helped you to the bedroom.'

'But I was naked.'

'You noticed. I took your clothes off. Thought it would make sleeping easier.'

'Did I put my wallet somewhere? Doesn't seem to be here.' I've checked my pockets. Nothing. Neither in my jeans nor my shirt.

'Oh hell. Did you have a jacket?'

'Can't remember.'

'Of course you can't. I'll call the bar, let's see – it's just after eight Sunday morning. It's too early now but later I'll ring. In the meantime you can stay here, if you want. But I really think you should go to the hospital. I can drive you.'

'Don't worry, I'll be okay,' I say not sure whether this will be the case but hoping things will work themselves out.

'You're taking a risk. Head injuries can mean concussion or even other problems. I really don't mind taking you to a hospital.'

'I really appreciate all you've done. I might take a walk. See if I recognise anything. See you soon.' I get up, put my plate, cup and cutlery into the dishwasher and wander to the door. I want to feel less like a burden and to give the woman space. She's done more than anyone could expect. I might even be a killer but I can't remember.

Chapter 2 Sunday

It's still somewhat overcast but the sun is sneaking through, making sections of the sky gloriously blue – almost an electric blue. I walk down steps and along the path to a gate, and then wander down a hill that curves as I try to maintain my balance. How women with heels negotiate the steep descent of this mini-mountain baffles me. I have no idea what suburb I'm in. Nothing seems familiar. I have no idea which suburb I came from. If Jackie and I both ended up in Bondi, it stands to reason that both of us live in a nearby suburb. Unless, of course, there was a purpose in my going to that pub, The Anchor, but the name doesn't jog my memory. When I reach the bottom of the hill, I notice that the road to the right snakes up another hill and curves sharply down the other way. I'm torn. Why doesn't anything seem familiar? I take the downward path to the left.

I think about Jackie again, a true angel. She tried hard to get me to visit the hospital but I more or less dismissed that advice and effectively told her not to fuss. Perhaps I'm being foolish. I will seek help if my memory stays unresponsive but I don't understand the urgency. I feel positive that it's all going to come good.

As I wind my way down the bend I see a couple walking hand in hand. Am I in a relationship? My mobile phone must be in my jacket, I assume, because I couldn't find it among the clothes I'd had at Jackie's place. Perhaps somebody had tried to call me. I continue on my trek noting the numerous blocks of units in this area. I'm obviously in a very densely populated suburb. Then I come to a junction and I can see the ocean in the distance. A beach must be near. I continue walking. The walk makes me realise I must be reasonably fit as it doesn't take anything out of me. I see signs with Bondi written on them so I guess that it's Bondi beach I'm heading towards. When I reach a road that appears to be a major one, I stop and gaze at the water. Lots of people are either sunbaking or paddling in the water.

When I get back to Jackie's flat, I find she's not there. She has left the front door unlocked so I'm not stranded. I go back to bed.

I wake to a sound in another part of the house. In fact I haven't explored the house in full so I'm unaware whether Jackie shares it with someone else, a girlfriend or boyfriend or just a flat mate. I get up and wander outside. I listen and realise there's someone in the kitchen.

As I start down the hall, I hear that Jackie's on the phone. I get fragments. I shouldn't be eavesdropping but I listen nevertheless as I stand close enough to hear but not so close that she notices me. She says, 'I didn't think it risky. He was nice and basically … unable to harm anyone. Uh ha, I get it but he needed help. And he's dishy. Right. I know that doesn't mean anything. Sure, I get it but everything's turned out fine. Anyway I have to go. Talk to you later.' She hangs up and I walk into view.

'Hi,' says Jackie, 'I just popped out to get some groceries. In an hour or so, I'll be able to call The Anchor. If we can't find your jacket, do you want to stay for dinner?'

'That's very kind of you but I don't want to impose. I hope the jacket and my wallet can be retrieved. Then I'll find out where I live,' I say, wanting to show I've thought things through.

Jackie smiles. 'Of course. But if you need to stay somewhere you can stay here.'

'I'm a total stranger to you,' I say. Jackie had changed before going to the shops and looks attractive in clingy jeans, a fluffy white top and heeled sandals. I hadn't taken too much precise notice of her appearance before but now I look closely. She is tall for a woman, very nearly my height, with auburn hair, alabaster skin and a curvy figure on a slightly larger scale than judged fashionable by what you see in women's magazines. I like what I see and wonder whether I have a lady myself, a girlfriend or lover or wife.

'I'm taking a big risk I know. If you kill me through the night I won't know about it the next day,' she says, grinning.

I have no retort. I smile and tell her dinner is on me, assuming of course I can find my wallet. I ask whether I can use her computer for some internet surfing and she shows me to a study where there's a desktop. She presses the power button and says there's no password, so I can use the computer when it's ready. She leaves the room, which I now notice is small and tidy. It's painted in a warm brown colour and furnished with a desk, chair, computer and filing cabinet. There are prints of flowers and water scenes on the wall.

Using Google, I check out a map of Bondi, which includes The Anchor and its surrounds. Looking at the map, I figure the house I'm in is situated in Bellevue Hill. I check out information about the suburb. Wow. It's a nice area and it makes me wonder if I live in a nice area. Maybe Jackie is rich or earning a decent salary to afford this location. Then again she might be renting. I should ask but it's probably inappropriate to be so nosey to a hostess who has acted kindly towards me. I can't check emails, as I need to know my name, account type and password. The hassle in losing your immediate memory is significant. Maybe I should go to a doctor sooner rather than later. But that would require details such as identification, health fund, home address, for starters, stuff I can't remember. Also I imagine I wouldn't be able to pay so unless it were an emergency, it would be foolish to visit any medical practice. I don't feel any pain so I figure a slight delay won't hurt.

Before leaving the computer I check some news sites to see what's new and if anything will trigger my memory. I discover there's a lot of bad news – refugee flights abroad, economic concerns, crimes. But nothing helps me remember what's happened to me.

***

At 1 pm Jackie and I rock up to The Anchor, which opens at 12:30 pm on a Sunday. Jackie approaches the bar. 'Hello Lloyd, I called before about my friend's jacket.'

'Right,' he says. He goes into another room and emerges with a jacket. 'Found it hanging on a peg.'

'Thanks,' I say and take it. I'm not absolutely sure it's mine but I take it anyway. What are the chances of two people forgetting their jackets in one night at the same pub?

Back at Jackie's place, I go through the contents. There's a wallet, a set of keys and a mobile phone, which needs to be charged. There are three keys. I guess a house key, a car key … and I have no idea about the third one. So I go through the wallet, which has a number of compartments. The first has a number of credit cards: an Amex with the name Nicholas C Hunter, and a Westpac-issued MasterCard in the same name. Next is an ATM card for the National Australia Bank. Strange that there are ATM cards for two different banks, but it's too early for me to question myself on this, assuming that I do turn out to be Nicholas C Hunter, of course.

The next compartment contains a Medicare card and a card from HCF, which could be from a private medical benefits organisation, I'm guessing, as it shows a membership number. The HCF card is for me alone, suggesting I'm single. But I suppose I could still be living with somebody. There is also some cash – $355. I see a zipped pocket at the back. I open it to find a driver's licence. This shows relevant data. There's a photo of me and the name Nicholas Hunter, so I know this is definitely my wallet. It also has my date of birth and an address.

'What's the date today?' I ask Jackie who is reading the Sunday newspaper at the table.

'It's Father's Day, September 6, 2015. Are you a dad?'

'I don't know but it seems that I'm thirty-four years old.'

'That's a start. And your name is?'

'Nicholas Hunter.'

'Well Nick, where to from here?'

'I own a car but I have no idea where I left it.'

Jackie looks amused. 'Do you want me to drive you around until your key unlocks a car?'

'Of course not. But if you'd drive me home, I should find some record of the vehicle.'

It turns out I live in Rose Bay.

Chapter 3 Sunday

We find a parking spot in the street in Conway Avenue, Rose Bay. I walk along the street with Jackie following. I locate the building from the address shown on my driver's licence and the flat number from the ground floor directory of this block of units. The building, from the outside, looks square – but once we're inside, the lobby appears freshly painted and inviting. The directory confirms the impression that the building contains three levels. I'm at the top according to details on the right-hand-side directory. We walk upstairs until we're outside a door painted black. I try the key I have. The door opens easily and I wonder whether I'll be greeted by a flatmate or a lover or a wife.

I walk in and invite Jackie to join me. To the left is a large kitchen/dining area. I look around. It's a modern kitchen. Painted all white, it contains an island with stools alongside, a large pantry and stove, and dishwasher and microwave units built in.

'Wow,' says Jackie, 'nice kitchen. Are you a gourmet chef?'

'I don't have any idea,' I say, walking through the living area and out onto a sun-drenched balcony. The view of water in the distance is marvellous.

'Lovely view,' says Jackie, 'You must be loaded.'

'Again, it might be an illusion. I'm probably renting.'

'One thing's for sure. You're no optimist.'

'Is that bad?'

Jackie laughs. I go back inside, through the lounge, and see an internal staircase, which I ascend. On the upper deck there's a study, a spare bedroom and a master bedroom that looks out over the bay. I live by myself, it seems, as there are no clothes in the closet except for a set of male clothing, suits and shirts and trousers, which I assume belong to me. The closet also has a large full-length mirror, which makes me wonder who designed the flat. A set of drawers on the other side of the room, opposite the long window, contains cricket whites, trainers and sunscreen.

Jackie is behind me. 'A lovely bachelor pad, it would seem. You must do plenty of entertaining of young ladies as I see no photos of loved ones.'

'Again, I'm in the dark. Hopefully my memory is only temporarily impaired,' I say, heading for the study. I'm hoping that there are records here that will help. I also plug my iPhone into a charger. Then later I can make calls or at least search for contacts.

'You hope your memory will return! You are taking a risk. I still think you should go to a doctor to check it out.'

'You worry too much. I feel okay. No pain at all. Also there might be a benefit in forgetting the past. I could have concerns which are enormous so not knowing might make dealing with everyday life easier,' I say, somewhat more tongue-in-cheek than I'm prepared to admit.

Jackie peers at me. We are standing side by side now. 'I did some rough research on the internet regarding amnesia.'

'And?' I say intrigued.

'I learned that loss of memory referred to as amnesia can be temporary or permanent and can be caused by head or brain injuries, drugs, alcohol or traumatic events.'

'That's great, Jackie. Now we both know it was a head banging. So it wasn't a traumatic event or anything. What did it say about a hit on the head?'

Jackie continues, somewhat exasperated by my attitude, I imagine. 'The severity of amnesia depends on the cause. Concussion seems to temporarily disrupt the electrical activity of the brain so it is likely your memory will return but when is the question.'

'That's good news. So I'll wait. I'm sure a doctor will probably say exactly that – to wait and see. Or suggest tests that will cost large amounts of money.'

'Can I help?' says Jackie, no doubt wanting to change the subject.

'Have a look in that filing cabinet for car insurance papers to tell me what I drive. I'll scour the stuff in the computer desk.'

'Okay. I'll try not to pry into anything too personal,' Jackie says, opening the top draw.

I don't say anything but suspect that people like to pry, no matter what they claim. I'm not sure why I should have this instinct but it's not memory, simply a natural perception of human nature.

After a few minutes, Jackie cries, 'Ah ha, I think I've found your car registration forms.'

'Fantastic,' I say, 'And what do I drive?'

'Wow. An Audi A6 sedan. That shouldn't be hard to find.'

'Let's go find it. It's probably near the pub.'

I climb into Jackie's more modest Honda Civic and we travel towards The Anchor. I feel better now that I know where I live and that I own a car. But is anything actually mine? Still I can't concern myself about that right now. I can go through papers and call contacts once I've found my car. My iPhone should be charged up by the time I get back.

It's turned into a sunny day, which now matches my mood. Didn't Jackie think of me as pessimistic? Isn't one entitled to be somewhat down if one has no identity, no place to live or no memory of anything?

We drive around the streets near The Anchor and eventually find a black Audi, in Sir Thomas Mitchell Road, with the number plates shown on my registration papers. I get out and test the key's remote button. Lights blink. It's the right car.

'Great news,' says Jackie. 'You now have a home and a vehicle. What next?'

'Dinner tonight?' I ask.

'Aren't you sick of me?'

I walk over and give her a hug. 'Absolutely not. Pick you up at 7 o'clock?'

'Okay,' she says and gets back into her Honda. I watch her drive off.

Before I get into the Audi, I check the vehicle's exterior to ensure that it hasn't been damaged. Then out of nowhere a man charges at me. He has an enraged expression on his bearded face and I think he has a knife in his hands.

Chapter 4 Sunday/Monday

The man coming towards me is a medium-sized bloke and he looks committed to do me damage as he's running hard to strike me. I don't know what to do and I obviously can't recall what I may have done to annoy this guy. Dressed in a dark brown jacket, dark jeans and thick black boots, he runs at me, knife pointed at my midsection. I weave and move in a way that surprises me. My hands are quick and I disarm him easily, instinct taking over. Then as he aims a punch, I avoid it and hit him hard, in the throat, and he is temporarily stunned. I follow up with another punch to the chin and as he falls back I administer a well-aimed kick to his groin.

As he drops to the pavement I'm ready, should he show signs of resistance, to kick him in the face, but he stays down. I collect the knife. Without further ado, I get into the car and drive away, wondering what brought on this attack. Was it random or was I targeted? I have no way of knowing as I examine the weapon. I put the knife in the glove compartment, wondering whether I should take it to the police for fingerprint identification, having wiped my prints off. But for the moment I focus on my driving, recalling the route Jackie used to drive from my place.

When I arrive home, I check my iPhone and see that it's charged. Luckily it's not the latest version so I don't need a code to use it. I open it and scroll down the contact list but I don't recognise any name as someone I know. Nothing triggers my memory. Perhaps I should go to the hospital tomorrow. But for some reason I'm reluctant. I'm not sure why this is, whether it's something deep seated, or instinct. In the meantime, I shower and change into some casual clothes.

That night, sitting across from Jackie at La Piadina in Glenayr Avenue, Bondi, I tell her about the earlier incident. 'Lucky to be here,' I say.

'What did the man look like?'

'He was a little shorter than me but stocky with a Ginger Beard,' I reply.

'Sounds like the man who attacked you last night,' Jackie says, frowning. 'He must have some grudge against you.'

'So what happened last night with this guy? Was I rude to him?'

'I don't think so. As I recall you went to the bar to order. I didn't take too much notice but it seemed you were standing waiting to be served and you turn around. I guess you must have heard something because the bearded man enters the pub along with other rowdy people. Then out of the blue this guy pushes you, follows you and using his fist knocks you down. My friends run over before he can hit you again and force this fellow outside. As soon as my friends let him go, he runs.'

'Sounds like a targeted attack, a bit like today,' I say, realising now that the attack was not random.

'We thought the bloke was on drugs,' says Jackie. 'So we forgot about it. Fights by crazed druggies happen far too frequently these days.'

The comments got me thinking. Had I annoyed somebody? Was I targeted by criminals? Was I in a criminal gang myself? This loss of memory was turning out worse than I could ever have imagined. But I am not about to admit this to the wonderful Jackie. She's wearing a low cut dress that shows off her breasts to good effect. I find her hugely attractive. 'Maybe I'm being paranoid?' I offer.

'How did you manage to overcome him if he had a knife?' asks Jackie, shutting the menu and putting it to one side.

'Look, I couldn't tell you exactly what happened. Somehow, something within me took over and I avoided the weapon and ended up belting him.'

'You're probably trained in some way. You might be a soldier or policeman, do you think?'

I also close my menu. 'Hell, I wish I knew.'

We order food. We eat the dishes we ordered in a leisurely manner, sharing them, not talking or thinking of my memory lapse. The dining and chatting is a pleasant experience. Outside the restaurant, I give Jackie a hug and kiss her on the cheek.

'Don't be a stranger,' she says, 'You remember my name, don't you?'

'I do and your number is now in my phone. It's the only number and name I can put a face to.'

She walks to her car while I watch. I want to make sure nobody has followed us and that nobody is going to harm Jackie. She gets into her silver Honda Civic and drives off. I get into my Audi, also checking that nobody is stalking me, and drive home. What a weekend.

After a sound sleep, I imagine, as I can't recall waking during the night, I open my eyes at seven o'clock on the dot, according to the bedside clock. Maybe my mind's programmed to wake at this time. I don't know. It must be Monday morning if yesterday was Sunday and I'm wondering whether I should report for work somewhere. But where? My memory is still impaired. I shower, shave and dress, the experience seeming novel in this place, which presumably is mine. I'd imagine Alzheimer sufferers find every day intriguing in much the same way. It's all a new experience again. That makes me think of parents. Do I have some in Sydney? Are they alive?

Breakfast is the next challenge. I look in the fridge. Well, it's not inspiring. A large jug of water, a carton of milk, two packets of cheese, four eggs and some butter. No bread. I shut the door and walk out. Wandering down the streets, I reacquaint myself with the area.

My phone buzzes. Fantastic, somebody knows me. I look at the caller id. It says Mark Bellmont. I answer, 'Hello.'

'Nick,' says Mark. 'How you doing?'

'Fine,' I say, not knowing who Mark is. A friend? A business acquaintance or a sporting buddy?

'Organised for Saturday?'

Damn. I have no idea what he is talking about. 'Remind me again.'

'Very funny,' he says.

'Humour me, I've had a tough weekend.'

'Your speech as best man for Andrew's wedding on Saturday,' he says.

'Oh that, still writing it. Better do it before the buck's party, hey?'

'Have you lost your mind? The buck's party was last week. You almost fell into the harbour on the cruise, if you recall. Get some rest, you need it.' He clicked off.

So what have I learned? I have friends, obviously one good friend if I'm supposed to be someone's best man. And I now have two contact names, Mark and Andrew. I look at my iPhone contact list and call Andrew Ford, the only Andrew on my list. 'Hi Andrew,' I say. 'How are you holding up?'

'Nick, I'm good. You've still got the ring, right?'

'Of course,' I say, realising I need to find this ring and not knowing where I hide valuable property. Using the notes section on my iPhone as Andrew is talking about his plans, I write a note to remind myself that I have to retrieve a wedding ring. Then I tell him how good the plans sound.

'So want to meet for a drink this week, before the big day? I know Megan is having some of the bridesmaids around to chat.'

'Sure. Where?'

'The Oaks in Neutral Bay. You know where we drink after cricket?'

'Sure, how about Thursday at 7 pm?' I say to buy time.

'Okay, see you then.' Andrew clicks off.

I've learned more about myself. I play cricket and I now know the name of the bride. That's a start. I plan to have breakfast then visit a local doctor. I find a café and sit down. A waitress brings a menu. I order bacon and eggs on toast and a cup of flat white.

'That's a change from your usual cappuccino,' she says.

'You know me?' A silly question but it escapes my lips before I can button them.

'Sure Nick, you're a regular for coffee.'

'What's your name?' I say.

'Julie. You're weird today.' The waitress walks off.

Back at home I wander around searching the place more thoroughly for clues of who I am and what I do. But more significantly I need to find that ring. The kitchen seems reasonably tidy with no pots and pans, uneaten scraps, unclean crockery or junk lying about. So either I'm a tidy individual or I hire a professional cleaner. I have no idea but I'm not going to fuss over that question too long.

I walk into the living room and see that there is a cream sofa, a black armchair, a drinks cabinet. Also a large-screen television and a table. On the table is a laptop. I hadn't noticed this before. It might contain useful details. I walk over and sit on the soft black leather chair and roll it close to the table. I open the laptop, a silver covered Lenovo, and press the on button. It warms up and then asks for a password. I'm stumped so I leave it and climb the carpeted steps to the next floor.

The bedroom has a large king-sized bed facing a built-in wardrobe with a full-length mirror in the middle section. I open the wardrobe to review what I own more thoroughly. I find suits, jackets and business shirts hanging above folded shorts, T-shirts and jumpers. Below this surface are pull-out drawers that contain socks, ties and underwear. All I can imagine is that I have an office job, as there is nothing that suggests working as a tradesman. Presumably I'm not into DIY which doesn't surprise me.

I open the top drawer to the bedside table and discover a Jack Reacher crime novel, some cuff links and a key. I wonder why it's not on my key ring but no doubt it will become clear soon. The lower drawer holds a camera, and a Harvey Norman Photo Centre packet with photos inside. I flick through the photos but there are few images of people. There is one photo of a young couple smiling. I turn it over but there is nothing written to indicate who they are. I put the packet back. I can study these later.

Next I visit the second bedroom. This room is tidy so it appears I haven't had a guest recently. It has a queen-sized bed as well as an empty closet. Finally I pop into the third bedroom, which looks more like a study. It contains bookshelves with plenty of books and some DVDs. Here I find a desktop computer, which makes me wonder why I also have a laptop. But rather than speculate I press the 'on' button and let it come alive. Surveying the rest of the room I see there is a single bed against the window. Perhaps this is for an extra visitor staying overnight who is not a lover. So I imagine I've had more than one guest stay over. When the computer has finally come to life I peer at the wallpaper of a beautiful woman. I can't remember whether it's an actress or just a picture I fancied. This computer needs no password to proceed. I play around and discover my memory for working things hasn't deserted me.

Running through the files I come across a file called 'Work'. I open this and realise that I must be a writer of some sort because there are plenty of articles and stories. Am I a journalist or novelist? Not sure yet. I try email and find I've sent material to newspapers so I must be a freelance journalist. I could have tried email on my iPhone but that didn't register when I looked at the icons. Well, that's something, knowing I'm freelance. Could explain why nobody from work has contacted me. I must work from home.

Then I open my photos.

Chapter 5 Monday

First thing I notice is that I've arranged the photos into folders by specific categories, and that beneath each photo is a notation citing details such as place, date and subject. I wonder for a moment whether I did this or whether I hired somebody to do it. But why would I hire somebody to go through my private photos? So I look at the categories more closely.

Folders are arranged in alphabetical order and are titled: America, Asia, Europe, Holiday 2009, Miscellaneous, Sydney 2008-2012, and Sydney 2013 with no end year. Does this mean I've travelled extensively? I'll catch up with the continents in due course but for now I need to check my recent Sydney photos to see who I know.

Oddly enough I didn't label the photos of people in this folder, presumably because I know them. Or else I didn't have time. I don't recognise anyone. There is a picture of an older couple, perhaps my parents. They appear to be in their fifties. They're smiling and look happy. There are individual photos and group photos. As the images don't help me, I leave them. I try the 'My Documents' folder.

This folder has headings such as Finances, Income tax, Travel and Work. I open 'Work' to discover that this file only contains completed assignments. Current work assignments must be on my laptop. I check a few folders to see whether I've recorded passwords. No luck. I'm stumped. Will I need to find a hacker to get into my laptop? It's disconcerting and I've lost patience.

I connect to the internet and using a search engine, I find the name and address of a local doctor. I call and make an appointment.

'Have you been here before?' asks the receptionist.

Of course I don't know but I say, 'No.'

I'm told I can pop in at two o'clock.

The Medical Practice on New South Head Road isn't hard to locate. When I arrive, I walk in to find a dark skinned receptionist with a lovely smile. She asks me to fill out some forms, which I do. I leave the previous illnesses section blank, as I have no idea what ailments I might have suffered in my past. When I return the completed forms I'm told to wait so I pick up a magazine on celebrity gossip, which I find amusing. Half way through, I'm called in.

The doctor is a white-haired gentleman called Benjamin Cranston. He shakes my hand, introduces himself and tells me to sit down. 'Now what can I do for you, Mr Hunter? May I call you Nick?'

'Sure,' I say as I glance at the wall, which displays medical certificates.

He's looking at me, waiting.

'I've lost my memory,' I say, not knowing how to deliver this news other than coming right out with it.

'That can't be good,' says the doctor.

'It's not.' I wonder whether he thinks I'm joking.

'Hmm,' he says, looking confused.

Then he takes my blood pressure and I can't see any connection between what I just said and what he's doing but he's the medical expert. 'Any suggestions, doc?'

'Blood pressure seems okay.'

'That's wonderful. What about my head problem?'

'Does your head hurt?' he asks as he prods my head with his fingers.

'No.'

'What happened? Did you fall and hit your head?'

I explain what Jackie told me at The Anchor.

'Well,' he begins, 'the brain is a peculiar beast and we don't exactly know what happens when you have memory loss. It may return soon or in years. There's no specific treatment that I'm aware of.'

Just as I thought. No need to panic except for the fact that I may have responsibilities of some kind and I have no idea what or if there's something important to which I need attend. But I don't say anything to the doctor about my personal issues. Instead I thank him and just as I'm about to go on my way, he says, 'I would strongly suggest that you see a specialist. Here.' He hands me a referral with the name and number of a Macquarie Street doctor.

'So you think I shouldn't wait and see?'

'Absolutely not. The fact that you can't remember is serious. I'd send you to a hospital but you've already waited too long and they'd just tell you to go to a specialist. Please take this seriously, Nick.'

I take a walk before getting into my vehicle. I want to explore this area. Then as I round a street, two men jump me. One is the same guy who previously attacked me, and this time he has brought a hefty looking mate with him. They punch and I feel a few body blows, but manage to step away and kick out. I land a foot on one man's chin and he falls. The other guy, Ginger Beard, comes close and I take his arm and wrench it back until he cries out in pain. I head butt him and he falls. The first bloke, hefty, is on his feet but he looks wary now. I wait. He comes at me and I duck, weave and smash my palm into his nose. He's gone. He collapses. I then rush and sit on top of Ginger Beard, my three-times attacker. I look into his eyes and aim my car key at one of them.

'Why are you after me?'

He smiles but says nothing. I thrust the key down. He screams but I've only dug into his cheek. 'Tell me or the next time it'll be your eye.'

'You agreed to write an article but you haven't. And you're not to mention Antonovich,' he stutters, looking fearful. I hit him again making sure he gets the message not to screw with me.

I leave ensuring both men are still down. Ginger Beard holds his face and gets up, gingerly. As I head to my car I wonder why I'm being attacked. To do an assignment? It sounds crazy. My employers would just issue a deadline and a follow-up message via email, surely. And what's with Antonovich? Did I write something about him? I'll need to break into my laptop.

At home, I try various combinations using my name and date of birth to determine a password but none work. Perhaps I should find some computer genius to break the code. But I don't know anyone. And therefore I can't trust anyone. I take a break and go out onto the balcony. As I look out at the blue sky I wonder whether I should call the police about the attacks on me. But I hesitate. I obviously have skills to cope with individuals attacking me. Am I into something which is dangerous that I simply now know nothing about? Do I have a criminal record? It's too much of a risk to expose myself to the cops at this point. I need to know more. Then I get an idea.

Back at the laptop, I type the street address number after my initials. Nothing. Then I enter my initials with the street number. Again, no success. Then I add my date of birth to the last attempt. Bingo, it works. It's running on a program I don't recognise. After trying some icons I get to a folder called documents. This only contains two items: Miscellaneous and Work. I review the Work section and find it's in alphabetical order. I must be a methodical sod. So I look at some documents that prove I'm a journalist of some kind. Then I go to the item with the latest recorded date. I open the folder called Ministerial Corruption.

I read the opening paragraph:

For a long time now Australia has had a clean slate in Parliamentary circles with respect to scandal and corruption. That has always been the province of the United Kingdom, which has had all kinds of scandals throughout its history. But now a prominent Australian MP, a Russian go-between, and a Middle Eastern terrorist organisation have combined. Names and dates and video evidence have been gathered, and the story can now be revealed.

I read on and it's abundantly clear that the story is not complete. And I had named Antonovich. But what of the other parties? Who are they and are they after me too? And why haven't they found where I live? Perhaps they have, it's hard to know. It's extremely bizarre. I need my memory, more than anything. Without it, I'm a sitting duck.

The other aspect of this partially written article I'm not sure about relates to whom I need to send it and whether there is a deadline. And how could I complete it without knowing what the hell it's all about? I search for notes but none seem to be available. I try Miscellaneous and come across a folder entitled Contacts. I open this and find some names. I match these with my iPhone and discover that some of these listed contacts are not on my iPhone's contact index. Interesting. Perhaps these are business numbers. Why aren't they on my phone? Why are they secret?

I'm not sure whether to try these numbers right now. I write them on a piece of paper so that I can write the name against each when I call. I close the laptop. Then a knock on the door startles me. I wonder whether it's another attacker. But why would they knock? So I brace myself and walk to the door. I look through the peephole. It's a woman. She doesn't appear to be carrying a weapon so I take the plunge and open up. Before me stands a petite individual with auburn hair.

I wait, smiling. I don't recognise her.

'Nick, hi. Where were you yesterday? Matt and I expected you for dinner. Did you forget?'

'Sorry, I got caught up,' I say, wondering whether I should mention amnesia.

'A new lady?'

'Yes, actually.'

'That's okay. We understand. I guess it's hard to find somebody like Linda again.'

I don't know what to say. So I had a girlfriend at one stage called Linda. Good to know. 'I really am sorry. It simply skipped my mind.' How well do I know this woman and Matt? Should I ask her name? But that would be stupid.

She turns and walks off. 'Come down for a drink tonight if you want.'

'I'll see,' I say. Then when she disappears downstairs I follow,

36

wanting to know whether she's from level 2 or level 1. She goes into a door on level 2. Right, she's a neighbour and she and Matt appear to like me enough to invite me over. I should make notes, I figure, but of course I won't do that. I return to my flat and consider my next step.

My iPhone buzzes.

Chapter 6 Monday

'Hello,' I answer brightly, hoping whoever it is will state his or her name.

It's a man's voice. 'I can't talk. Meet you at the usual place six o'clock tonight?'

Shit. Who is this and what is the usual place?

'Remind me about the place,' I say.

'Why?'

'Maybe I have a few places where I meet people.' I hope I sound convincing. He might think me peculiar but I'm prepared to accept the stigma.

'Wynyard Park in the city, second bench on the right.'

'See you there,' I say, wondering whether I'm agreeing to be murdered. But the city at that time would be crawling with people. Peak hour for commuters. I guess I'll be safe enough.

I reread my current article and examine my emails to see if I can reconstruct the assignment. But I have no luck. Finally I give up and go outside with a beer. Luckily I'd bought beer on my way home from breakfast. I sit on a comfortable chair on the balcony to contemplate my life. Looking out to the bay, things appear great. I have decent accommodation, a fine car and a new friend, Jackie. I seem to have a job and a social life, but because I can't recall how to continue my project or who my old friends are, I count these things as a negative.

I research Wynyard Park online and work out how to get there. I take a bus. At five minutes past six, I walk along the footpath, looking for the bench where I'd agreed to meet the mystery guy. When I spot somebody on the right bench, I proceed. As I approach I observe my surroundings. There are tons of people queuing at bus stops. Also, there are many men, women and teenagers in business and casual gear walking along the paths. Everyone seems to be in a hurry. People keen to go home after a hard or boring day in the office. I look around and see a pub across the road. Surely that would be a more congenial meeting place. But I stand near the bench and wait. I check the time. Six oh-seven per my mobile phone.

Mystery man looks like a regular office worker. White shirt, open necked. Navy slacks. Black shoes, unpolished. He is a thin and frightened looking individual, glancing this way and that. When he sees me he looks directly at me. There is no smile. So he's no friend. I sit beside him, not knowing what to call him. Do I shake hands? He doesn't offer his so I presume not.

I look at him. He wears glasses and his hair is sparse. He's about forty-five or fifty. Hard to determine because he looks so serious. He hands me a newspaper. 'This is the last of the stuff,' he says. He gets up and strolls away. I have no idea what's just happened. Still I'm alive, so I should be grateful. No assassin, this thin scared man. I look at the newspaper. Is this how I receive my daily news of writing requirements? Bizarre. I examine it further and realise there is a file hidden inside. So this is what this is all about. My contact moves off, blending in with the crowds. I go home the same way I came. By bus.

At home, I review the file. It contains information about the MP I have been writing about. So this is my 'deep throat'. Great. I can continue my article, I guess. But I'm hungry and it's dinnertime. When I shopped earlier I'd bought some basic items. I make myself a steak and salad. Then I sit down and read the file again. It has damaging information about corruption involving an MP, Muslims, and a Russian middleman named Antonovich. After having read the contents fully, I decide I need a break.

I visit Matt and his auburn-haired petite wife on level two, bringing some beer along. I might learn more about myself, so it's probably a useful thing to do. I knock on their door. A moment passes before the woman appears. When she sees me she smiles and ushers me in.

'Hey, Nick,' says Matt, getting up from the sofa. He's watching the large-screen television set mounted on the wall. 'How're you doing?'

'Good. What are you watching?'

'Some dumb reality program. Ann loves these shows.'

Ann says, 'You watch them too.'

'Ann tells me you have a new girlfriend, which is why you stood us up. You sly dog, you,' says Matt, looking more upbeat than annoyed.

Perhaps he likes the idea of a bachelor spreading the love, something many married men probably dream of. I say, 'Sorry about that. Slipped my mind.' What else could I say?

'But Matt, we haven't seen Nick for a while so who knows how many ladies he's seen?' Ann giggles.

Matt grabs the remote and clicks off the TV, accepts the beer I brought and gets a bottle opener. 'How come you always buy these fancy European brands? Aren't Aussie beers good enough for you?' he shouts from the kitchen. 'You need an opener to drink these.'

I ignore the jibe. Did I buy Heineken from instinct because I don't know what I normally drink? I look around and see that the layout of the unit is different to mine. For a start everything in their flat, including the bedroom or bedrooms, is on the same level, with no internal staircase. So the lounge/kitchen area is smaller than mine. The place looks well maintained, probably Ann's doing, but I'm guessing.

I'm invited to sit down. I choose a leather armchair and wait. Matt comes back, hands me a bottle, and then sits down opposite me with a Heineken as well. He places his beer on the coffee table, which is positioned between us. Ann joins Matt on the sofa with a glass of white wine.

Matt is a short wiry fellow who regales me with events at work. He is a salesman and he enjoys telling stories, it seems. Then he says that he'd invited one of his colleagues over for the Sunday dinner I missed.

'And,' says Ann, 'I invited Brenda over on Sunday as well. She reminded me of Linda.'

'Really, how so?' I say taking a swig from the bottle. I like this beer.

'Brenda looks a little like her. You know, lovely skin, and quite slim with straight shoulder-length blonde hair. But she's nicer. Not short-tempered like Linda was.'

'So you were trying to set me up?'

'No,' says Ann, suppressing a smile.

'Of course you were,' says Matt, glancing at his wife. 'You can't let a single guy enjoy himself.'

'Have you seen Linda since we split?' I ask, trying to get an idea of my ex.

'Not a word and I thought we were friends,' says Ann.

A little more chat and I say I have work to do. I stand to leave, shaking Matt's hand, and then extending a hand to Ann who kisses me on the cheek. I guess I know this couple well.

Back in my apartment I run through my emails again to find a connection between the title of my article and the publication for which I'm writing. Finally, after reading a number of 'sent' emails, I find a likely contender. I make a note to call in the morning.

Chapter 7 Tuesday

I wake early the next morning. It's a bright day, with a light blue sky evident when I open the blinds. I eat breakfast but hold off on coffee because I prefer to walk to the café just so I can chat to my regular waitress, Julie. But before I go I wonder whether it's too early to call Maxine Short, the woman with whom I corresponded about a newspaper piece. I call a mobile number, one that I tracked when Maxine replied to my email. The email didn't say much, certainly nothing pertaining to the type of assignment, the money or the deadline. All it said was that it acknowledged my story and that I could get in touch if I had any questions.

No response. It's just after eight so maybe Maxine sleeps in.

I descend the stairs then wander outside, taking a deep breath, wondering what the day has in store for me. I take a seat at the café after ordering a cappuccino, which is what I usually have according to Julie, who had smiled at me as I'd entered. Julie is around twenty with a trim figure fashioned by regular gym work, I guess. She's wearing spandex tights, which accentuate her youth and vitality. She also sports a reddish ponytail. She has a pointed face and a ready smile.

When Julie brings my coffee over she says, 'Are you more yourself today, Nick?'

'I guess,' I say.

'Had a rough weekend, I imagine. Too much partying?'

'Too much rough living, ageing me before my time. And why are you always so chirpy?'

'Oh, I don't know. Just me,' she says, sauntering off.

It feels good to have a routine and to be recognised. I hope

I don't have to start off like this with everything. I need my memory back but there doesn't seem to be an available and immediate remedy. I trudge off up Dover Road after my coffee, watching people closely in case somebody wants to harm me.

At home I try Maxine again. This time I get a response.

'Hello,' says a female voice.

'Maxine?'

'Yes. Who is this?'

'It's Nick Hunter. You spoke to me about an assignment?'

'I did but you can't talk about this. Meet me at the Quarryman's tonight, say seven-thirty.'

'Okay,' I say, and click off.

I check out what and where Quarryman's is. According to Google it's a pub in Harris Street, Pyrmont. I note the address and work out the best way to get there by car.

At 7:20 pm I'm seated in the main bar. I won't be able to recognise Maxine so it's best she approaches me. I order one of their twenty-odd craft beers on tap and wait. At around 7:40 pm, a woman with black frizzy hair stands beside me. 'Hello,' she says, 'Can I buy you another?'

'Sure,' I say.

She orders two beers. She suggests we sit in the corner where it's more private. I follow her. Even in black high heels, she is a head shorter than I am and dressed in a white blouse and pinstriped trousers. She is thin, her voluminous frizzy hair making her head appear large atop her body. She looks about forty and has the appearance of a high-level executive. We sit opposite each other.

'Nick, you know the article is highly sensitive implicating an Australian Member of Parliament and a Russian criminal. Why did you want to speak to me on my mobile, which may be under surveillance?'

'Sorry,' I say, not really knowing how to tell her I know little about anything. 'Just wanted to check the deadline.'

Maxine screws up her nose. 'Is that all?'

I want to ask what the assignment is about but stay quiet. I take a good few gulps of beer hoping she will disclose more.

She says, 'You still have a week and a half. We'd like to include it as a Sunday feature in three weeks.'

That sorts out the deadline. 'Thanks, that's what I thought,' I lie. I want to ask how I got the job and whether I had to sleep with her to get it but, of course, that would be indelicate. And I imagine that the approach to do the story may have come from me, given the leak from the guy in the public service.

'Is your government source giving you all the information?' Maxine says. She sips some beer, seemingly not enjoying it the way I am.

'Oh yes, that's going okay.' How would I know? My work hasn't progressed enough for me to understand what I'm aiming for in the piece. 'But the Russian connection isn't going well,' I say, wondering whether this has significance.

'I thought you knew someone or went undercover. If your cover's blown you could be in strife.'

'Tell me about it.' Was I undercover? How? Why? I'm a journalist not a criminal. Jesus, there's a lot I have to find out.

'It'll be a mind-blowing article,' Maxine says, putting her hand over mine as though I'm a child needing reassurance. 'An MP bribed to allow uranium sales to the Middle East through a Russian middleman. Your work might inspire a movie. How do you feel about that?'

'I feel … ' I start, but I can't go on. I drink more beer and say I need to go.

On the drive home I drop in to see my only current friend, Jackie.

'Hello, stranger,' she says when she opens the door. 'Come in.'

'Thanks,' I say, following her into the kitchen where she puts the kettle on. I think of myself as a stranger too, now that I think about it. I know so little about myself and I seem to have so much going on. A wedding is looming. It appears I work undercover for a criminal. I'm

44

writing a major newspaper article on corruption. What else?

'So have you been to the hospital?'

'I saw a doctor. He informed me that my memory may return but he has no idea when.'

'Is he a specialist?'

'No,' I say, realising that the answer is stupid. The doctor made sense. Will a specialist prescribe a pill to cure me? I doubt this but it's a thought. 'However he's given me a referral to see one.'

Jackie takes out a couple of cups from a cupboard and places them next to the kettle. 'Good, that's a start. Coffee or tea?'

'Coffee, please.'

She serves the hot drinks and sits opposite me at the kitchen island. 'What have you discovered about yourself?'

'I seem to be some sort of journalist. I have a regular coffee place and a few bits of other stuff. There's still a lot I need to find out.'

'It must be exciting, finding out who you are,' says Jackie. 'I know who I am and sometimes I wish I were someone else.'

'You don't mean that.'

'No, not really. But there are those moments when life gets a bit much and you wish you could start over.'

'Is that how you see my situation?' I ask.

'You have no choice but in a sense you need to start over, don't you?'

I look at her penetrating eyes, which hide an intelligence not always evident. 'Yes. But I suspect I could be in danger from what I've learned recently.'

'Do you want to stay here tonight?' she asks, grinning.

'I'd love to but not under these circumstances.'

'What's that mean?'

'Not as some poor lost soul,' I say. 'Only as someone you've chosen. Which raises a question I've been meaning to ask. Why haven't you got a partner or boyfriend? You're not a lesbian, are you?'

Jackie laughs. 'Wow, what a question to ask someone. Obviously you're out of touch with privacy laws or more to the point forgotten all about them. But to answer your question – no, I'm not a lesbian. And as to male companions, I've never met anyone with whom I've had a proper rapport.'

'But you've had lovers?'

'I have. Are you now going to ask how many?'

'I wouldn't dare.' I have to admit I'm pleased there is nobody romantically linked to her at the moment. Still I'm uncertain how to proceed. Perhaps I should have taken the stay-the-night proposal. I'm discovering I'm fairly hopeless in the Don Juan stakes.

'So what now?'

'It's late. I'd better go.' She walks me to the door where she pecks me on the cheek.

It's late Tuesday night and as I walk up the stairs to my flat I sense somebody is outside my door.

Chapter 8 Tuesday

Yes, when I walk another few steps I see a figure, confirming my assumption. It seems to be a blonde woman. Is she the assassin I'm expecting? I walk another few steps and then I can see the person clearly. Definitely a trim blonde woman who appears to be pacing back and forth. Then she bangs on the door. 'Nick, please let me in.'

I walk further and when I'm on the same level, I say, 'What's your problem?'

'Oh Nick,' she says, 'Thank God. I thought you weren't going to let me in.'

'Why should I let you in? This is my flat.'

She smiles. She appears intoxicated. 'I know, silly. But I did live here too if you recall,' she says rather sarcastically.

'Linda,' I say, guessing.

'What's wrong, don't you recognise me? I haven't changed that much in seven months, have I? I've put on a couple of pounds but that's all.'

'No, you haven't,' I lie, not recalling that this woman had been part of my pre-amnesia life.

I realise it's late and that there's no point in talking in the hallway. And as she's not an assassin, I should be safe if I let her in. I open the door, usher her inside and ask if she wants coffee. No way am I going to invite her to have more alcohol. After all, maybe we parted because she was an alcoholic.

She knows the place as she stumbles in and flops on the sofa. 'Thanks, Nick. That would be nice. You haven't changed. Manners –

something I've always liked about you.'

Perhaps I can learn more about myself. This woman may know me better than anyone. 'So what brings you over tonight?'

'I was down the road with Rodney, having a few drinks, and we got into a terrible argument and I just left and I wanted to see you. I miss you.'

I bring coffees over and sit opposite her. I'm not sure I like this woman. But I must have, once. 'Who's Rodney?'

Tears well up. 'He's … ' she slurs.

I wait. I hope she isn't going to cry. I'm not sure why but I don't like this show of emotion.

'He's my boyfriend but after tonight I don't know that we'll be able to carry on.'

'A bit like us?'

Linda tests the coffee. 'Not at all. We parted because you were away so much.' She wipes her eyes.

'I don't recall that,' I say. I'm probing for information now because she may think I'm playing games, and I'm not going to tell her my condition in case she feels sorry for me and wants to reconnect. I can't imagine wanting any part of this neurotic female.

'Really. You've said numerous times you had to travel for work. Often you were away for weeks without any contact.'

'So why did you stay with me?'

'You were kind and intelligent,' she says – and then, with a grin, 'And good in the sack.'

'But you left anyway,' I say, still not sure why we broke up.

'When you returned from your overseas jaunts you wouldn't tell me what you were doing, that it was confidential and best that I didn't know,' she says, fully coherent now, the past no doubt flooding back.

'Maybe I was writing about sensitive issues.'

'Don't pull that one. You did something else.'

'Did you suspect I was having an affair?' I don't know what else to say as I can only guess that I would not have revealed the information she needed because the subject of my trips was confidential.

'Perhaps but not really. You were always pleased to see me when you returned so I didn't suspect anything of that nature. And you did call me occasionally. So I was mystified and then I became angry when you had to do more trips.'

'And did I say where I went?'

Linda peers at me like I'm some kind of idiot. 'You know perfectly well that you didn't. There seemed to be something strange you were into but you wouldn't tell me. Can't you tell me now? Now that we're not together? Now that I regret leaving? And I want you back, you dumb bastard. I still love you.'

I'm taken aback. She loves me. Surely I went away to escape her neurotic nature. Maybe she too was good in the sack and I could only put up with her needy personality for a brief time before having to escape somewhere. But that doesn't seem plausible. I'm sure I had legitimate overseas assignments and that I was asked not to reveal too much. But how would I know? 'Linda, I'm sorry if I caused you so much hurt. I really am. But the past is the past.'

'Why can't you confide in me? I thought we were going to get married.'

I'm shocked. 'Well … what can I say?'

'We lived together for nine months and we managed a nice life when you were around.' Linda is suddenly touching my hands.

'Look, I need my sleep. I have a deadline I need to meet. Perhaps we can talk more later,' I say. I really want her gone. My life is simply too complicated at the moment.

Linda gets up and staggers to the door.

'Sit down. I'll call a cab,' I say with more authority than I've had since the head bang. I don't want her driving or even walking around in her soporific state.

Then when she's gone, I wonder what the hell I'd done. Had my trips abroad anything to do with the Russian criminal? I doubt it. What Linda was talking about was ages ago, surely.

I'm about to go to bed when there's a knock on the door. I check my watch. It's 11:45 pm.

Chapter 9 Wednesday

Who would call at this time of night? I know Linda has gone because I'd helped her into a taxi. Concerned it might be a disreputable person, I grab a long sharp kitchen knife and walk to the door. I peer through the peephole. It's a guy holding a bottle of wine. Does he know me? Did I party late with friends in the past? I open the door, hiding the knife behind me.

'You're not Janice,' he says.

'I hope not,' I say. 'You may have the wrong building.'

'Sorry,' he says and disappears.

I must be getting paranoid. I'm jumpy at every sound or unusual sight. I have to calm down and think rationally. I can't live in a state of constant fear. It's wearing and I'm tired.

I go to bed.

When I wake, on the dot of seven o'clock, I feel refreshed. Now that I know I have a deadline, I jump into the shower after shaving and brushing my teeth, have breakfast and set out to work. I re-read the unfinished article and review the material from my source again. Then it hits me. The Russian go-between wants the Australian MP exposed but he wants to stay in the shadows. It seems, from the documents I have just obtained, that Antonovich is a businessman connected to politicians and Australian suppliers of uranium to the Middle East. And for some reason the MP involved is doing a secret deal with Antonovich. This explains why the guys wanted to threaten me by beating me up or injuring me to keep Antonovich's name out of the media, but not kill me. Killing me would kill the story as well.

I need to know more. Something doesn't make sense.

I stand up and stretch then go to the mailbox. Inside I find a pizza flyer, an electricity bill and a credit card statement. Back inside my flat I look at the credit card statement closely because it may give me more clues about myself. The balance, in excess of $6,000, makes me realise that I need to find out about my financial health. I also need to find out which bank I do business with. God, it's all too hard. I contact the specialist I've been referred to.

I make an appointment with Dr Albert Birnstein for the next day at noon. In the meantime I need to relax. So I decide to go shopping at Bondi Junction, a nearby mall I discovered when researching the area on Google Maps. The internet is a wonderful invention.

I get to Bondi Junction and find a huge underground car park. As I walk up the escalator to the mall, I recall some of the items on my detailed credit card statement. Food from Woolworths, fuel at Caltex, items from a clothing shop, Foxtel, a telephone charge and a large amount at a place called Minx. I'd looked this up and it was a Gentlemen's club in Pitt Street. I can't fathom why I went there or who might have been with me.

Oblivious to people walking past, as I'm looking at the shops, all of which seem new and glamorous, I'm startled when someone calls out to me. It's Jackie.

'Hi,' I say. She looks glamorous as well. Dressed in a figure-hugging black mini skirt and print top, she appears to be going to the races. 'I thought you worked.'

'I do. I'm a hairdresser and I'm going to buy some lunch. Would you like to join me?'

'Sure.'

We find a café and order coffees and sandwiches.

'How have you been? Any improvement in the memory department?' she asks once our orders have been taken.

'No, no progress on that front. But you'll be pleased to know that tomorrow I have an appointment with that specialist I mentioned,

51

recommended by a Doctor Cranston.'

'That's great news. Have you received calls from family and friends?'

'A call from a friend. I'm best man at a wedding on Saturday apparently. I don't know how to handle it except I'm meeting the groom-to-be tomorrow night so maybe more details will come to light.'

'No call from a lady friend or friends?'

'No, Jackie. Looks like I'm single and not committed,' I say, intrigued.

The coffees and sandwiches arrive and we consume them while chatting about the mall, since I know nothing about it. Jackie points out that the place is relatively new, renovated and refurbished over a period of years. Then she looks at her watch and stands up. 'I need to get back to work. Would you like to come over for dinner tonight? I make a mean spaghetti bolognaise.'

'Okay,' I say, wondering why she's inviting me over. Is it because I don't appear to have a girlfriend?

Later, wandering around, I buy some things to take to Jackie's. I remember where my car is parked and drive back home. So my short-term memory after the knock on the head is intact. It's been a good day so far with nobody attacking me. I sit in front of my computer and examine my financial folder. First up, I want to take a look at my account with the National Australia Bank using the information on the card I found in my wallet. I check Miscellaneous and find a file with passwords. I'm set. I can use my credit card, the ATM and other things. Oddly the password for my laptop is not included.

The night is cool and I don clean jeans and a casual, collared blue T-shirt. I select a suitable blue checked jacket and some slip-on shoes. When I arrive at Jackie's at seven o'clock, I hand her red roses and a box of chocolates. She seems pleased and invites me to sit on the sofa. Jazz music is playing on her sound system and she hands me a beer, a Peroni. No doubt she took notice of the beer I had at The Anchor.

She joins me, sitting beside me on the sofa, with a glass of white wine. 'Do you feel disoriented because of your condition?' she asks.

'No. Just weird. I have to think about every step I take. I'd imagine when you remember stuff, a great deal of what you do comes easily.'

'Like what?'

'In your case you know where you work and you simply go there each morning. You don't have to find out what you are and so forth, if you see what I mean.'

'Yes, I get it, although the routine can get boring.'

I move closer and kiss her on the lips. She doesn't resist. I put my arms around her and feel my trousers swell. After a long passionate kiss I release her. Then I kiss her neck. She responds by pushing me over on the sofa and lying on top of me. She kisses me on the lips, first gently then using her tongue to explore my tongue. It's not long before we discard our clothes. Before we can take maximum advantage of this situation the doorbell chimes.

Jackie hastily slips back into her dress, pushing underwear under the sofa while I flee to the bathroom where I get dressed. When I return to the dining area, Jackie introduces me to John and Louise Harrison. 'These are my closest friends. You met them at The Anchor.'

I shake John's hand and nod to Louise. John is fair haired and around my height, six foot, but Louise is short, around five foot four and very skinny.

'Have you recovered from the bump on the head?' Louise says.

'Yes,' I say. 'I had bit of a headache the next day.'

'I bet you did,' John says.

We all sit down and Jackie organises a beer for John and a white wine for Louise.

'We're sorry to intrude,' says Louise, 'but we were in the neighbourhood and wondered whether you'd like to come to The Anchor for a drink and something to eat.'

'Thanks for the invitation,' says Jackie, 'but I have spaghetti bolognaise ready and there's plenty so you're welcome to join us.'

I feel a little let down, as I want to continue with Jackie on the sofa, where we left off. I hope the couple decline.

Louise looks at John, who shrugs. 'We'd love to,' Louise says.

Not much later the four of us are sitting around Jackie's rectangular wooden dining table. I don't know what timber it's made out of but it appears solid and varnished to appear almost stately.

'This is great,' John says, tucking into the meal.

'Very nice,' Louise adds.

Not to be outdone, I say, 'Superb.'

The conversation revolves around food and I tune out. Instead I look at Jackie who is wearing nothing underneath her long flowing dress and I find it difficult to concentrate on my spaghetti. I picture her as she was before the intruders arrived. Lovely sheer white skin, ample breasts, which I had touched only momentarily, and a curvaceous figure. I put my implements down for a moment, savouring the experience I had almost had.

'Something wrong with the dish?' Jackie asks.

'Not at all,' I say. 'It's delicious. May I have a top-up of the fabulous red wine?'

'Of course.' Jackie pours more Brockhill Merlot into my glass, the only empty one.

'Did you hear about Rhonda?' Louise asks.

'No, do tell,' Jackie says.

'She's so desperate to get married, she's applied to get onto that *Married at First Sight* show.'

'Really?' Jackie says.

John and I continue to consume our spaghetti and wine while the women talk about people they know either getting married or wanting to get married.

'And you, Jackie,' Louise says, brushing a strand of her dark hair from her face, 'you'll need to get hooked up soon. Particularly if you want children.'

I look at Jackie, who blushes.

'Rubbish. I'm in no hurry.'

The evening continues for hours with a dessert of strawberries and cream, coffee and chocolates, and more wine. Finally, around midnight, the visitors depart. I'm relieved but feel somewhat awkward now. Do I simply say that we should adjourn to the bedroom or offer to help wash up? I wait for Jackie to indicate what she wants to do.

'It's late,' she says.

'Wonderful meal. You went all out.'

'Not at all. I love to entertain. But I need my beauty sleep as I have to get to the salon early tomorrow.'

'Right,' I say, 'Can't tell the boss you're not well, I suppose.'

'I am the boss,' she says, 'I own the place and I have a new hire starting tomorrow. So I have to open up and get the joint tidied.'

I stand. 'It's been great. I need to go, too.' I have to make her feel that she isn't the only one being responsible – which she is, of course.

We embrace and kiss goodnight and I can feel her body under the flimsy dress and I want to ravish her right there and then, but I also want to see her again and I act like I don't care.

'See you,' I say, and leave.

On the drive home, my iPhone buzzes. I pull over and take the call, as I need to know who my friends are, assuming this call is from such a person.

'Hi Nick, it's Jill. You said you were going to call.'

Chapter 10 Thursday

I'm stunned. So I have a girlfriend after all. Or was Jill a one-night stand?

'Sorry,' I say. 'It slipped my mind. I've been very busy with work.'

'But you work from home. At least that's what you said,' she responds.

'Anyway Jill, I've been off the air. Tell me again what I promised.'

'You said you'd call me. After our great night at the Ivy last Friday I thought you'd be real keen to see me again. It's now late Wednesday and I can't wait by the phone any longer. What's going on?'

'Are you free tonight at 9 p.m.? I'll be at The Oaks in Neutral Bay,' I say, to get her off my back. Better confront her than brush her off by phone. Besides, she might be fabulous. I still haven't slept with Jackie so I don't think I have any obligation to stay pure should I be tempted otherwise.

'Okay, I'll see you then.'

This also solves the problem of wanting to know what she looks like. She'll approach me. Perfect. I click off. I have a big day coming up – the doc, the groom-to-be, the possible girlfriend. At home I hit the sack and sleep comes easily.

I wake at 7 am recalling my last dream in which I was seated, tied up, with Jackie, Linda and Jill teasing me by performing lap dances. We were all naked. The hot water from the shower snaps me out of this scenario, albeit exciting yet scary, and I think of what I need to do today. After a breakfast of eggs on toast and coffee, I sit down and focus on the article. Whatever point I originally wanted to make is foreign to me. I'll have to start from scratch, using the material I currently have. It then occurs to me that I must have been given stuff by my informant previously. I retrieve the key I found a few days ago and look at it closely. It might be a safe-deposit key. I pocket it. I phone the bank to discover where my local branch is. I'll pay a visit later, I promise myself.

After drafting notes for an approach to the article, I take the bus to the city and walk to Macquarie Street. As I walk along I'm blown over by the magnificent buildings and I note that Macquarie Street leads to gardens, which, from my research, must be the Botanical Gardens. What a wonderful city. I should explore it sometime soon. I find the address, admire the impressive stone structure and go inside. I check the directory and take the elevator up to Birnstein's level. I advise the receptionist of my appointment and the thickset middle-aged woman gives me a form to complete.

Dr Birnstein invites me in after a short wait and I produce my referral. Birnstein is a short wiry man with hair on the sides of his scalp but none on top. He points to a chair on the side and I sit on it. After examining the documentation in front of him, he walks around his desk and peers at me. 'How does the head feel now, Mr Hunter?'

'Not bad. I haven't experienced any headaches since Sunday morning. Where did you get the letter from?'

'My colleague who referred you. He gave me some details about you as well as what you told him,' Birnstein said, pushing his spectacles higher.

'What do you think?'

Without answering he comes over, and using his fingers examines my skull, prodding here and there.

'Well?' I ask, given that he has done the job, walked back to his desk and jotted down some notes.

'Nothing obvious can be detected. But, given that you have no lasting headaches, I want you to have a brain scan. First, let me tell you about myself in case you're thinking of dismissing what I'm suggesting.' He looks at me to ensure I'm paying attention. 'I'm a qualified neurosurgeon and have performed operations for some years. I'm also one of the top people in my field of expertise. I have worked here as well as in the United States. I'm now a consultant for this practice but I have lectured on the topic of head injuries at Sydney University. I've seen many different types of head traumas but yours intrigues me.'

'Why is that?'

'It seems you've suffered from a physical injury yet you don't appear to have the classic symptoms. Which is why I'm recommending a scan. Here, take this to the address shown and I'd suggest you have it done soon. Then I need to see you again.'

'Should I make an appointment with your receptionist today?'

'That won't be necessary. We'll call you. I want you to take this seriously. Some people who feel no pain ignore medical advice and find out when it's too late that they suffer from a condition that might have been caught early and successfully treated.'

I put the piece of paper in my jacket pocket, thank the doctor and leave.

Next I walk down Bridge Street to George Street. The National Australia Bank building is a tower of immense proportions and is confronting as I walk towards it. It sits on the corner of George Street and Grosvenor Street and looks modern and must be thirty or more floors high. I enter the lobby through revolving doors and, after finding the bank client service area, ask about safety deposit boxes. I'm told that the bank that holds these is at another branch, up the road at 343 George Street. I feel foolish but don't let on that I can't remember much.

When I finally reach the right bank and section, I provide appropriate identification and gain access to my safety deposit box. A woman in her thirties, quiet and non-talkative, takes me to my box. The key I brought with me works in conjunction with the key given to me by another bank employee. I open the box. Inside I find a passport, a Smith& Wesson M&P 22 Compact pistol, and a large brown envelope. The envelope contains papers and on cursory examination they relate to the article I'm meant to write. I take the envelope and place it on a table to take with me. I peruse the passport. The photo is of me but the name of the passport holder is not Nick Hunter, it's Dmitry Takovich.

At home, I read the details of the data in the envelope. The details are scary. The article I started has little of this material included. Perhaps I needed the second instalment to integrate all the bits into the story. I find the name of my source and a contact number. I need to call this guy. The information is too explosive to accept at face value. But I must have accepted it when I had my memory. Still, the new me cannot write the story without some proof that it is genuine. Because if it is false I would be condemning a key parliamentary minister as well as leaving myself open to libel.

The contact name in the government is Donald Murphy. I call his number. No response. I work on the article, vowing not to provide any of this to the newspaper until I can verify the details. I wonder whether I had been this sceptical previously but then again I have nothing to compare any earlier impressions with, given my current situation. The brain scan may reveal how I should proceed. I'd made an appointment for next Monday, the earliest time available.

Until I leave for the Oaks, I sit and listen to music. I want to reacquaint myself with what I like. I run through some of the CDs I own and select one by Ellie Goulding. Somehow I fall asleep and find it's nearly six o'clock when I awake.

I call Murphy's mobile number again but I'm greeted with voicemail. I leave a message. I get ready for the evening, a prospect that excites me but not one I'm actually looking forward to.

Chapter 11 Thursday

The Oaks Hotel in Neutral Bay is situated on the corner of a busy road and finding parking had been a nightmare but I'd persevered. In the end, I'd had to walk a number of blocks along a street called Military Road to get to the pub. At least it gave me a chance to familiarise myself with the area. Double storey and triple storey buildings line the road with stores, bank fronts and cafes among the most prominently displayed entities. A true busy suburban village. Cars rattle along slowly as the traffic is dense from commuters travelling home after a tiring day in the office or factory.

Entering the pub, I look around and after getting to the head of the queue at the bar I order a schooner of Tooheys New, the first tap I see, and debate where I should wait. Carrying my beer carefully to avoid bumping into bodies roaming about, I sit on a stool facing the entrance. It is 6:50 pm and I trust Andrew is not early. Nobody seems to have recognised me so I expect I'm safe. I sit and watch people. Groups of men and women laughing, couples staring into each other's eyes or drinks, lone men on the prowl and women in pairs chatting and probably waiting to be approached. I note one brave young man wander up to two women who are talking to each other. The tall brunette with tight black slacks looks at him dismissively as he speaks. Her companion, a short dirty-blonde woman wearing a dark skirt, smiles but says nothing. The tall one says something and the youth turns and walks off. A tough business attempting to pick up women this early in the night.

On the dot of seven o'clock, a tall lanky guy in shorts and a brown T-shirt enters and waves. I'm about to signal to him when I note he isn't looking at me but behind me. I continue drinking my beer. Finally at ten past seven, a muscular man in blue shorts and a black T-shirt with the word Ninja written on it approaches me. He smiles. 'How you doing, dude?' he says.

'Okay, dude,' I respond, not knowing whether this is the usual way I address my mates.

'Can I get you another?' he says.

'Sure,' I say. I watch while Andrew saunters to the bar. He is broad shouldered with brown hair and he's sporting a two-day growth. He seems comfortable in here, chatting to the barmaid serving. The place is filling up with more people arriving. It's noisy and I wonder how to direct the conversation. Perhaps I should relax and let Andrew take the lead.

The tall brunette I observed minutes ago is only a few tables away. She smiles at me and I don't know why. Surely she's not interested in me walking up only to be sent away with my tail between my legs. Andrew returns.

He places a glass in front of me and takes a huge gulp of his beer. 'Got your speech about the lovely bridesmaids sorted?' he begins.

'Tell me more about them,' I say.

'You know Sarah. She's Megan's younger sister and is a bridesmaid along with Katie, who's a cousin or something and you may have met her at one of our functions. But you may not know the maid of honour. Her name is Jasmine and she's hot. You'll love her and you might get lucky. But you don't need to worry about individuals, you just have to say how terrific the trio looks. Piece of cake. Of course you can say whatever else you want about me. You know all my secrets during and since high school so you might want to keep some of the darker stuff secret.'

'Oh really, like what?'

'The stuff you, Mark and me got up to, you know, raiding the girls' tents on camp and so on. I'm sure Megan doesn't want to hear about that.'

'Of course,' I say, realising that I'm lost for anecdotes.

We have more beers and I let Andrew do most of the talking. Finally, when it's close to nine o'clock, I ask him whether he's nervous.

'You're kidding. I've been living with Megan for three years. The mystery has gone. Plus she's preggers.'

'Congratulations.'

'Keep it to yourself for the time being,' Andrew says, swallowing the last of his umpteenth schooner.

'Sure.'

'Another one?'

'No thanks. I'm meeting someone else soon.'

At that moment, a dark haired woman walks up and smiles at us. 'Hi,' she says, 'I'm Jill.'

Andrew shakes her hand. 'Andrew,' he says. 'I'm just going. See you Nicky boy.'

'See you,' I say, turning to my new companion. Jill is trim and has nice short hair. She's wearing a dress barely covering her bottom with heels verging on the dangerous should she be required to run. She is relatively flat chested, which is interesting since I like Jackie's fully developed boobs. So why did I get involved with Jill? I'm waiting to see how this pans out.

'What have you been doing?' she asks, peering intently at me.

'Working,' I say, 'And you?'

'Me, too. I've had a number of deadlines crunching numbers but I managed to get everything done despite the lack of support. The stress is something else.'

'It's good to keep busy,' I say, wondering whether I should know where she works and the relationship she has with work colleagues and bosses. She may have told me and now expects me to understand the troubles she's having.

'Why haven't you called like you promised?' she asks, apparently keen to get this matter off her chest.

'Sorry,' I say, wondering what happened that evening we met to make her so keen to follow up. 'I have deadlines, too.'

'I understand but I thought we had a connection when we were together and you did say you'd call a few days later. Admittedly we were both three sheets to the wind.'

So who am I really? From what I've discovered about myself, nothing would make me want to get to know myself. I flirt with women, get drunk and act irresponsibly. I have a fake passport, own a gun and I've visited gentlemen's clubs. I've made enemies, serious enough for them to want to kill me and I live in a fine apartment in a prestigious suburb as well as get around in a luxury car. Am I a criminal? Or worse? But as I have no inkling, I have to get on with life as is. 'What can I say Jill, I'm probably a bastard.'

'You don't know?'

There is silence while I consider my next move. I note that the tall brunette is chatting to a good-looking man in a pinstriped suit while her companion appears bemused.

Eventually I say, 'Shall we go into the Bar & Grill section for a meal?' I'm hoping she'll decline so I can disappear.

'Okay. I haven't had dinner so that'll be great.'

We move to the garden and I follow her as she is tottering on her impossibly high heels, making unbelievably slow progress. Without the heels she'd be very short, around five foot two, I'd reckon.

We sit and review the menus. 'Anything take your fancy?' I ask.

'You're so polite. Not like your boisterous self at the bar where we met.'

'Really? Do tell.'

'You were pissed. I was a little too but we got on great guns. Remember?'

'Vaguely,' I say, realising this would be true whether I had amnesia or not. I feel surprised that I seemed to have been an extroverted guy. I don't feel like that now.

'You were loud and funny. Tonight you seem to be quiet. Have you gone off me?'

'I've had a lot on my mind recently. Let's order.' And we did.

Steak and chips comes for me and for Jill a salad. I wonder whether she likes salad or simply likes to control her weight. At least Jackie has a hearty appetite. As we eat in relative silence, I wonder why I'm thinking of Jackie.

'Who was that bloke you were talking to when I arrived?' Jill asks.

'He's getting married on Saturday and I'm his best man.'

'Who are you taking?'

'Nobody.'

'Were the invites done ages ago?'

'Yes,' I say not knowing for sure how things had progressed. She's probably wondering whether she can come as my plus one but I have no intention of asking her. It seems I've only just met her and I hardly know anything about her.

We finish our meal and I want to pay and go. I don't want to cause any ill will and I'm not sure how to let her down gently. 'Did you enjoy your salad?'

'It was okay. Any dessert?'

'If you want some that's fine but I need to go. I'll take care of the bill.'

Jill looks hurt. 'Why do you want to leave? It's still early.'

'I have a deadline tomorrow and I've got a lot of research to do,' I lie.

'All right but when can we get together again?'

'I'll call you,' I say, wondering why she's trying so hard to corner me.

'Can you at least give me a lift home?'

'Okay,' I say. I can't very well abandon her. And she can't walk far, not in those shoes. 'Where do you live?'

'I'm starting to worry about you. You dropped me off when we shared a cab the other night after the pub party. It's a flat at the end of New Beach Road, Rushcutters Bay.'

We arrive outside her place thirty minutes later, half the time taken for her to waddle to my car in the shoes from hell. I have to admit she is alluring in those heels. She puts her hand on my thigh.

'Pop in for a coffee?'

I succumb. Why not? But once we're inside she attacks me by sitting on my lap. We kiss and she begins to strip. My mobile interrupts us, Jill left dangling with bra and knickers exposed. I still have my clothes on. 'Sorry,' I say, 'It might be important.' And it is. It's Donald Murphy, my very own "deep throat".

Chapter 12 Thursday/Friday

I walk to the far side of the small lounge room, watching Jill, who is almost naked, standing beside her sofa. 'Yes?' I say into the phone.

Murphy says, 'You called me. You know not to contact me unless it's an emergency.'

'Right. Well I can't really talk now but I need to meet with you.'

Jill gathers her clothes and storms off. The apartment has a balcony and I move outside. The stars are out and everything would be wonderful if I didn't have this conflict between Jackie and Jill and the call with Murphy right now.

'Impossible,' says Murphy and I can sense annoyance.

But I don't care about his feelings. 'It's important if you want me to continue.'

I can imagine Murphy's blood pressure rising and the veins in his neck thickening as he virtually screams, 'You have all the information and you must do what you promised. Write the piece. Do you know the trouble I went to, the difficulties I had, the danger I'm in?'

Of course I have no idea about anything that Murphy is experiencing as I watch the moon in the distance. Also I don't really give a toss. Life is becoming unbearably complicated and I don't like it. The view from here is beautiful, lights twinkling, water swelling ever so slightly, and I want to just sit down and stare at it. I also see a few boats rocking in the water and wonder whether nearby residents own these vessels or they're simply moored in this idyllic part of the city by others. 'Shut up,' I hear myself say. 'See you at Wynyard Park tomorrow at noon.' I hang up. I look at my watch. It's nearly midnight.

I go back inside and find that Jill is not around. I leave. She'll probably be in a poor mood and the last thing I need is to deal with somebody else's bad mood. I get home, enjoy a glass of Johnny Walker Black Label Scotch Whiskey, and then undress and slip between fresh sheets.

In the morning I visit my local café and have breakfast. I enjoy eggs Benedict, orange juice and a cappuccino. Julie comes back to clear the table and asks what's in store for me today.

'First thing I've got to do is find a wedding ring since I'm best man at a wedding tomorrow.'

'How could you lose something like that?'

Julie is wearing fitted jeans and has her dusty blonde hair in a ponytail. I look at her smirk wondering whether she thinks I'm a hopeless case. 'I don't know but I've lost the damn thing so I need to do a thorough search this morning.'

'I hide special stuff in my sock drawer.'

'Who do you hide it from, parents or boyfriend?'

'My flatmates,' she says, indignant.

Later at home I rummage through my sock drawer. No luck. Then I try other drawers. Just when I'm about to give up, I try the pockets in my suit jackets and casual jackets. And there it is, in a jacket pocket. It must have been given to me one night and I didn't remove it. I could kiss Julie.

I take the bus to the city and arrive at Wynyard Park just before noon. I get to the designated bench and sit down, trusting nobody else wants this particular one. It's a beautiful cool sunny day and great for enjoying a walk or just lazing in the sun. But I can't relax. Not until I question Murphy. I check my watch. Twelve-ten. Impatient, I call his mobile. No response. Finally after waiting another fifteen minutes, I realise he's not coming. I call again but the result is the same and I curse.

Wandering around the city I reacquaint myself with the streets, buildings and shops. I get to a one-way street called Pitt Street and walk south until I come to another one-way street with traffic heading east. I cross when the lights allow and arrive at a pedestrian-only mall. This appears to be the central shopping district of Sydney. High-rise buildings stand on both sides, their entrances leading to arcades and major department stores.

When I get near the end of the 'people only' stretch of pavement, I encounter a huge sign shouting the word 'Myer'. Escalators ascend or descend, carrying people higher or lower yet I choose the spiral stairs, which take me down into a food hall. I buy a coffee and a healthy bran muffin and consider my options. People are everywhere, queuing at counters, walking about and seated at the many tables provided. The crowds are amazing. I'm pleased I work from home rather than commuting and being swallowed by masses of humans jostling against each other and lining up for positions or seats for lunch or on transport.

Back at home I google Donald Murphy. Some names listed as Donald Murphy appear but none who work for the Department of Defence. There are some professional people with that name listed. One chiropractor and one urologist as well as an actor but no one remotely likely to be the man I'm after. Then a thought occurs. I google my name. But as the name is not uncommon I find plenty of men with that name. I try the LinkedIn tab which advertises the top twenty-five Nick Hunter profiles. I scroll down until I find a rather dated photo of myself. Although the photo is not flattering I can't complain. It does the job. I review my profile, which says I'm a freelance professional journalist, writer and editor. I live in Sydney – good to know. I was educated at Sydney University. That's it. Not very comprehensive.

All I know about Donald Murphy is that he works in Sydney for the Department of Defence as an administrative officer. I should be able to track him down. I spend time on the internet and the phone to search for Murphy. But no luck. I wonder whether he actually works there. Perhaps I took the information on blind faith. That doesn't make much sense. In my pre-amnesia days, I would have checked his credentials, surely. Anyway I leave that particular problem for now. I take my laptop and write a best man speech for tomorrow. This takes an hour or more and when I finish I check the time. It's twenty past six. I'm hungry, ready to eat the leg off a cow.

I look in the fridge but there's nothing inspiring in there. A pizza washed down by beer would do the job. I google pizza for Rose Bay. A knock on the door disturbs my focus. I wander to the door in jeans and bare feet. I'm about to look through the peephole but realise I probably wouldn't recognise the person anyway so I open up regardless. A pleasant surprise faces me. It's Jackie.

'Hi,' she says, 'are you doing anything tonight?'

'No,' I say, 'Come in.'

She walks through to the living room and turns around. 'Here,' she says, handing me a bottle of red wine. 'I thought you may be at a loose end since you can't remember things or people.'

'Thank you. Very thoughtful of you. Please sit. I was just about to order pizza. What do you think?'

Jackie, seated on the sofa, screws up her face. 'Typical bachelor food. Why don't we go to an Italian instead?'

'Sounds good to me. Let me get changed. I'll put on some music.'

'Don't worry. I'm happy to just sit and admire your prints on the wall. I didn't get a chance before. Did you choose them? Oh, forget I said that. You wouldn't know, of course.'

I change into cream slacks and a black shirt. I take the bottle of red and lock the door once Jackie is outside. We walk to New South Head Road and into Grandfather's Moustache, an old-fashioned Italian restaurant in a modern setting. There's a sign saying 'No deliveries. No credit cards' but the place is packed. I'm impressed at how the restaurant manages a busy clientele without compromising its own standards. After being shown a table, I look at Jackie. 'You're a lifesaver. Didn't you have plans?'

'Of course. But I cancelled them all.'

I take Jackie's hand and brush my lips across her fingers. 'I guess you'll just have to make the most of an evening with a memory challenged person.'

'Tomorrow will be a test for you.'

'The wedding. Yes that should be fun. I'd invite you but I think it's not possible now.'

Jackie leans back as the waiter delivers drinks. 'Naturally. Besides, I won't know anybody.'

'Join the club.'

Jackie laughs. I like her sense of humour. The evening goes smoothly. We eat a shared pizza and enjoy the wine. Jackie tells me she came to Sydney from a country town in western New South Wales. Her parents and younger sister are still in Coonabarabran but she says she's happy to have left. We have coffee and then walk back to my place. At the foot of my block Jackie says she enjoyed the night. I suspect she is going to get in her car and drive off so I put my arms around her and pull her close. We kiss, a long lingering, passionate kiss. Her lips are soft and I want her to swallow me.

'Come in for a nightcap?' I ask when we disentangle.

'I have to work tomorrow,' she says, without much conviction.

I take her hand and lead her to my apartment. She doesn't resist. She also doesn't object when I take her into the bedroom and disrobe her. She then does the honours on me and soon we are facing each other stark naked.

A phone rings but we ignore it. I push her on top of the bed and climb over her and after a moment into her. Because of my extreme lust I don't last long. However I sing in my head throughout the activity: 'I love you because you make me feel so alive'. So when I roll over I take her in my arms and tell her to wait for a short time so I can give her total pleasure. Less than thirty minutes later we make love again, this time in a slow measured fashion, then both of us fall asleep. I don't ask whether she enjoyed it. I know I did.

At around four-thirty in the morning I go to the bathroom. On my way back I check my mobile. I had a missed call from a mobile number that I don't recognise. I wonder whether this was from Murphy or from someone attending the wedding. I will deal with this later. I return to Jackie who is warm and half-awake. I stroke her and she becomes fully awake. This allows us to repeat what we'd done earlier.

Chapter 13 Saturday

At ten past seven I wake to find Jackie missing. Had I dreamt being with her? No, I didn't dream the events of the night before with the luscious Jackie. I can feel one part of my body that has been thoroughly exercised. I lie back and relive parts of our association and feel grateful that my recent memory is intact. I get up and wander to the en-suite bathroom. After freshening up, I go back to the bedroom and dress. I remember the missed call and wonder who would have called so late on a Friday night. Then I delay calling until after breakfast.

It's eight- thirty and I imagine most people should be out of bed by now so I place a call to the number from last night. I wait for a few rings before it is picked up and answered by a sleepy voice. 'Hello, who is this?'

'Good morning. It's Nick Hunter. You called last night?'

'Yeah mate. Look, just wanted to touch base about today. Want to meet for a drink beforehand?'

I don't want to drink with some random guy. 'Remind me where the church is again. I think I lost my invitation.'

'We didn't get one, remember? Andrew just told the details to us groomsmen. The church, it's the one in Normanhurst, you know, at the college where Megan went to school.'

'Okay,' I say. I realise it's best to meet this guy as I need help with the time and location. 'Where do you want to meet?'

He tells me a time and place. I have a few hours to get ready if I'm to meet him at three. He hasn't told me his name so it'll be interesting but at least he'll be dressed in a suit so I should be able to pick out the right guy in the pub. I expect the wedding is scheduled for four or five o'clock.

Walking into the Pennant Hills Inn just before three, I feel idiotic. The few patrons inside are in shorts and T-shirts and I'm kitted out in a black suit, polished black brogues, stiff white shirt and a yellow tie. I look around but the guy I'm supposed to meet isn't there. I buy a schooner of light beer and sit on a stool. Five minutes later a slap on my back alerts me to my friend's presence.

'G'day, mate,' he says.

I turn and see a solid man of around thirty. He's grinning. 'Hi,' I say. 'Can I get you a beer?' He nods and tells me his preference and this gives me time to think of my next move. I deliver the beer and then another groomsman walks in.

'Hello, Nick. Hi, Ian,' he says.

'G'day, Gary,' Ian says.

What super timing. Ian, the beer gut, and Gary, the tall streak of misery. Now I have images that I shouldn't forget.

We chat about nothing in particular for a while, enjoying the beers. Gary mentions the weather, Ian the last cricket match. Then Ian says, 'Tonight, after Andrew and Megan leave the reception, let's take the girls somewhere, hey?'

'What did you have in mind?' I ask, not sure whether this is our usual behaviour.

'Not sure yet,' Ian says, 'but we should make a night of it. I hear that Jasmine is hot.'

'I've seen her,' says Gary. 'She's fabulous. Bumps in all the right places.'

'She might have a boyfriend,' I suggest, not happy with how this is going.

'Nah, Andrew told me Jasmine, Sarah and Katie are all single chicks.' Gary smooths his lapel.

The conversation drones on and I wonder whether these guys are my friends as well as Andrew's. They may belong to the same cricket team but that doesn't necessarily make them my friends. Then at three forty-five, we leave for the church.

As we walk to our vehicles, I'm told Loreto Normanhurst is a private Catholic school for girls. There's a long driveway leading up to the chapel in which the service is being held. I park the car and walk up the steep curved pavement to the entrance. Ian and Gary join me and we seek out Andrew, shaking hands and making jokes.

The ceremony goes smoothly with me standing, transfixed by the lavishness of the event and the mass of invitees. It appears that Megan's family and friends outnumber Andrew's by a margin of two to one. I cannot believe that there are countless hundreds sitting on the pews awaiting this entertainment. Megan arrives on time, which gives me little opportunity to assess the bridesmaids. Brides are meant to be late, aren't they? I'm keen to examine the women thoroughly but at this stage can steal only cursory glances. They all look pretty in their blue outfits, long dresses with plunging backs. If the plunges were in front instead, it would stop the wedding. I can hardly wait to gaze at these women later on.

The priest does his piece, the couple say their words and I hand Andrew the ring when it's called for. Then we trudge outside, Jasmine accompanying me, behind bride and groom. She has a broad smile, flawless skin and a slender busty figure. She is out of my league. I won't bother trying to win her over as she is probably hit on by too many males to count. I'll let Ian try his luck.

Outside, the bridal party have to pose for photos. I do my best to smile when asked. All this palaver so that a couple can shag with the consent of society leaves me cold. Perhaps this is why I'm presumably still single. After the photo shoot, Ian approaches. He says, 'See what I mean about Jasmine?'

I look at him. What does he think? 'She's nice but not my type. Go for it if you want.'

'Don't worry buddy, I will.' He walks away, no doubt dreaming about his encounter with her.

People start to move to their cars. I follow Gary who knows where the reception is being held. Turns out it's at a place called Dockside in Darling Harbour. As I wander to the entrance I see many people already inside the venue, sipping glasses of wine or champagne. I grab a glass from a passing waiter and feel isolated. I don't know anybody. Should I seek out Ian and Gary? Then a man comes up to me and says, 'Hi Nick, did Don Murphy give you what you were after?'

I look at this guy for a moment, stunned. He is a fair-haired man of around forty with a thin moustache. He wears spectacles and has a slender physique. I don't know whether he is a friend or an associate. I reply, 'Not everything. I've been trying to make contact. Do you know how I can get in touch with him?'

'You have his mobile, don't you?'

'Sure but he's not responding. Have you got anything else?'

'I used to work with him in the public service and he got in touch with me first, as you recall, because I knew Andrew had a journo mate. But I only have his mobile number.'

'Why did he seek a journalist?' I ask, knowing that this question might sound odd.

'Don was raging about certain injustices but he wouldn't tell me what they were. I asked why doesn't he go to a newspaper and he said the information was too sensitive for just anybody.'

I sip some champagne. 'So how did you get onto me?'

'When I said something to Andrew about Don having a big story about people's frustrations with politicians, he came up with your name.'

'Okay. Well thanks for that but I can't finish my piece unless I can verify a few details. And Murphy won't return my calls.'

Andrew's moustachioed mate nods and takes out his Galaxy phone. He investigates something then turns back to me and says he has an address for his public service colleague. I take the information down on my phone. Murphy's friend then begins to talk about Andrew and he asks me how I know him.

I wonder whether I should make up a story but this is fraught with danger if he's a close friend of Andrew's. Pondering how to avoid saying too much, I'm saved by the lovely Jasmine who joins us. I excuse myself and take Jasmine to an area where we can talk.

Chapter 14 Saturday

'Thanks for rescuing me,' I say when we are in a corner overlooking Darling Harbour. At least I'd never met Jasmine before so I can speak with her without worrying about any past we may have shared.

'You're welcome,' Jasmine says. 'I need you to rescue me now.'

'Okay,' I say, noting the wonderful fragrance of her hair. She has shoulder-length chestnut hair and olive green eyes. With high heels, she is a few inches shorter than I am. 'How can I help?'

'Ian is hitting on me and I was hoping you would stay with me, like a partner. He doesn't have to know that we've never met.'

'Sure, I'll be happy to stick with you. Let's get another drink.' I say. I collect two glasses of champagne from another passing waiter and hand her one. 'Here's to tonight.' We clink glasses.

'Megan told me you're a journalist.'

'Yes, that's right. I'm a freelance journalist. And you?' I want to get off the subject of me. We both look out at the dazzling lights of the surrounding bars and restaurants. We are shoulder to shoulder now, occasionally glancing at each other.

'I'm a flight attendant. I've worked for a number of airlines including British Airlines and Emirates.'

'And which is your favourite?' I look at her as she sips her drink.

She laughs, a full throaty sound. 'I've never thought about it. I'm not a passenger, I simply attend to people's needs so it makes little difference.'

At that moment the crowd starts to move and I hear someone

from inside the venue asking for all to take their seats. Jasmine and I join the fray and take our place at the bridal table. I see that the tables have nametags so that everyone has a place and chaos is avoided. Andrew looks at me and winks. I smile back. I'm nervous, worrying about my speech with no foreknowledge of anecdotes or lives lived.

Meals are served and I see Ian eyeing Jasmine. Sarah is meant to be his partner in this event. Sarah seems nice. Young and a little on the plumpish side but with a pleasant personality from what I can gather. Katie on the other hand, who will no doubt be Gary's dance partner, is dark haired and tight lipped. She is the tallest of the bridesmaids and has yet to smile.

Then the speeches begin. The Master of Ceremonies, a small man in his forties with lots of nervous energy, asks everyone to be quiet, wielding the microphone like a magic wand. After explaining why we're here, as though anyone could forget or not know, he calls on the bride's father to get the process underway. The bridegroom, bride and the groom's father follow, all giving heartfelt speeches. Then it's my turn. I stand and survey the multitude of faces, all eager to hear about Andrew.

I start by thanking the bridesmaids, then I congratulate the bride and groom for entering into a lifelong deal of extraordinary opportunity for happiness, not mentioning that there is an equal opportunity for lifelong misery. Then I'm stuck. I can't recall the speech I wrote only recently and it seems dumb now. So I say, 'Andrew always had taste. I've only known him for a few days.' This attracts laughter. 'But he chose me as his best man so he knows something I don't.' More laughter. 'And I trust his judgement in selecting Megan as his bride. She looks fantastic and will no doubt make a lovely companion.' I ramble on some more not really knowing what I'm talking about but the audience seems appreciative. Finally I propose a toast. Everybody stands and the guests raise their glasses in unison.

The ordeal over, I sit down and sigh with relief. Jasmine looks at me and gives me an up signal with her thumb. At least she liked it. The dances begin and soon I'm dancing with Jasmine who seems happy.

Probably because she's escaped Ian's grasp. Then we sit down again.

Eventually Ian comes along and says to Jasmine, 'Dance?'

'Thanks Ian but Nick is about to give me a ride home. Sorry.' She pouts.

I'm taken aback but I do see an opportunity to escape and avoid difficult situations from people I should know. 'Yeah mate, we need to get going,' I say.

Ian gives me a strange look then slinks away. Jasmine farewells the other bridesmaids, and the bride seems put out that Jasmine is leaving before her. I slap Andrew on the back and make the right noises. He's not fussed with our imminent departure and tells me he'll see me at the next cricket match. I imagine he figures sport is more important than ritual.

'Nice car,' Jasmine says when we finally reach it through the maze that is the parking garage.

I open her door and she slides into the Audi's passenger seat, lifting her dress to reveal long sexy legs. I don't let my gaze linger so that I don't come across as a pervert.

We drive to Jasmine's place with her providing directions. I have no idea where we're going and I hope I can find my way back to my flat. I make a comment about this and she brings out a street directory from the passenger side. 'You have this,' she laughs, 'doesn't the car have a GPS?'

'I guess not,' I say wondering if I chose not to have one.

'You can always use your mobile phone,' she says as she returns the directory to the side pocket. 'I haven't used a street directory ever.'

'I'm a journalist,' I say, wondering what she is driving at. 'I like to flick through pages.'

The rest of the drive goes quietly apart from directions Jasmine gives in a sultry voice. I stop the car, turning off the ignition so I'm not indicating impatience. She then says, 'Your directory isn't current.' She laughs.

'But you have the latest mobile, I presume.'

She places her hand over mine. 'I'm joking. I think it's sweet, you being a little old fashioned.'

'Really?'

'Thanks so much, Nick. Would you like to come in for a coffee?'

Coffee. What does this mean? She's just being polite, I imagine. She's grateful that she's escaped the clutches of Ian who had been staring at her most of the night. 'I need to get up early tomorrow but thanks anyway.'

'Oh come on, we left early. You won't turn into a pumpkin. Come in,' she insists.

'Why not?' I didn't have a coffee at the wedding reception so I'm entitled. I follow her to the second level where she opens the door along a row of three flats. Inside I note she is untidy with clothes and shoes strewn about.

'Take a seat. I'll make us a nightcap.'

She brings me a scotch and appears to have spirits in her glass as well. She tosses off her heels, which land halfway between the television set and the sofa, and sits next to me cross-legged.

'Why did Ian scare you so much? You could have had a dance,' I say.

'He reminds me of my stepfather who had Ian's build and was a real arsehole.'

'Why? Did he abuse you?'

Jasmine plays with her hair and then looks me in the eye. 'My mother and father divorced when I was eleven. I loved my dad but mum got custody. When she remarried it was to a man I hated on sight. He thought of me as someone he could order about. Then around thirteen he tried to corner me and put his hand up my skirt. I fought back and told my mother who said I was lying. When I was fourteen I'd had enough and went to live with my dad. So I've always been wary of men who usually have one thing on their mind.'

'I see,' I replied, taking a sip of my scotch. 'I guess with your looks you've had to fight off men most of your life.'

'That's right. And in my industry, the sex is pervasive. Pilots and flight attendants are always having parties and after some drinks some of them are right into it.'

I don't know what to say. She has revealed too much about herself so quickly. So I mumble, 'So you've built up a resentment against men?'

She leans forward and kisses me. Her tongue seeks out mine and I move closer and she embraces me but I keep my hands to myself. After a full minute or so, she disengages herself and says, 'Not all men.'

'Why am I different?'

'I don't know. You don't seem predatory. I guess that's it. You haven't made a pass at me all night.'

Maybe I don't find you attractive, I'm about to say. But that's not true. She's very attractive with those big eyes, lovely porcelain skin and soft curves. But I'm still somewhat resistant because of Jackie, I think, and I don't know why that is. Does Jackie mean a lot more to me than a rescuer? 'Maybe I'm shy,' I end up saying.

'You're too good looking to be shy. Let's go to the bedroom.' She stands and pulls me up and I comply. I am led to her large bedroom, which is also untidy, but what do I care. The bed is large and soon we are undressed and my instincts take over. As we're touching and kissing each other I lose all sense of conscience, if I ever had one, and go with the flow. Who knows, I may be dead tomorrow, if not from an attack, then perhaps from a traffic accident. Enjoy this, I think, before letting myself sink into the blissful essence of the moment.

When I awake the next morning I remember the night before. That is a plus. And I check. The person beside me is Jasmine. I slide out of the sheets and grab my clothes. I'll get a shower at my place, I figure, rather than spend more time here where I could be tempted again.

Jasmine wakes as I finish dressing. 'Hey,' she says, 'I thought we might go out for brunch.'

'Sorry,' I respond, 'I have work to do.'

She makes a disappointed sound. 'It's Sunday.'

'I had a great time and I'm really sorry but I have to chase a lead.' I return to the bed and kiss her on the cheek. She pulls me closer and kisses my lips.

'Call me,' she says as I leave.

I don't respond and I have no idea whether I will or not.

What I have to do today is visit the elusive Donald Murphy.

Chapter 15 Sunday

I drive away in the luxury car I still cannot believe I own, thinking about what had transpired. It had been a weird outcome, considering the fact I had no intention of winning Jasmine. Perhaps my sheer indifference to her made me a challenge. I will never fully understand what happened or her motivation to seduce me. A puzzle but I have more practical puzzles to resolve today. I switch on some music and complete the journey to Rose Bay thinking about my mission.

At home I shower, change into casual clothes and eat breakfast. An orange, eggs on toast and coffee. Ready for my visit to Murphy I check the address on my phone, the one my nameless friend from the wedding gave me.

After twenty minutes in light Sunday traffic I reach the stated address, somewhere in Redfern. There is a black Mercedes parked in front of a single storey semi-detached house. I park a few houses away and walk to the timber gate. Before entering I look both ways to ensure there is nobody in the vicinity. I walk cautiously along the short path to the door. The place has a white brick frontage, a corrugated roof and vertical steel bars over the solitary front window. I'm about to knock when I hear voices.

One voice says, 'What do you want me to do?'

The second voice says, 'He's your choice. Tell him what you want reported.'

Voice one responds, 'He's a journalist. He'll do it his way. That's what they call integrity.'

Voice two explodes, 'The notes you gave him shows my name.

I know because I have a copy. You fix it, I don't care how, or you'll pay. Understood?'

I move to the window and see Murphy cowering. He nods. The other man is tall and strong looking. I leave hurriedly and hide behind a tree a few houses to the right of Murphy's place.

The tall black-haired man comes out a few minutes later and I watch him stride out the door with purpose and get into the Mercedes. He seems to be in his thirties and he is wearing dark trousers and a black short-sleeved shirt. All in all, he appears to be a dark figure. I wonder if this is Antonovich. I run to my vehicle and follow the Mercedes. In the light traffic I keep a fair distance behind the Mercedes but still need to drive quickly to keep up. We drive through streets and highways and over a huge bridge I don't recognise. After twenty or thirty minutes the Mercedes turns into a side street. I drive cautiously but try to keep my distance. He uses a remote to access a garage to a two-storey house, which looks well maintained and expensive. I drive past, noting the number. Then on the way back I look at the street name.

After driving a short distance I go to a café called La Piato for a coffee and, using the street directory I had in the car, examine the area. I discover that the man I followed lives in Mitchell Street, McMahons Point. My cappuccino arrives and I look about. People are entering. Groups and couples but no singles. I see from the time on my iPhone that it is around lunchtime. Being a Sunday, it must be family outings for most. I try to gather my thoughts.

It would seem that Murphy will contact me to dissuade me from something or to suggest a direction for the piece I'm supposed to write. So at least I don't need to chase him. But what should I do about Antonovich? I really don't know so I drink my coffee and peer at the people chatting and ordering drinks and food. With the back section of the restaurant half full, the noise is considerable. It looks like a good place to bring Jackie. I call her.

When a sleepy voice answers, I say, 'Are we up yet?'

'Of course. I'm just having a lazy Sunday in bed, reading the papers and playing games on my iPad.'

'Sounds great.'

'So how come you're so chipper?'

'I'm not really. Would you like to go to an Italian restaurant tonight in North Sydney?'

'Why not? What time will you collect me?'

'Six-thirty.'

Back at home, I review the material I have from Donald Murphy. After what I'd observed in Redfern, I'm suspicious of it. Is it reliable? Am I being played? I make notes of key aspects of the information so that I can check it against other data. I wonder what integrity checks I'd made when I originally obtained the material. At the end of my work I have a beer and sit down in front of the television. Looks like I have a set-top box that records shows, so I scrutinise what I'd recorded. It intrigues me. What was I keen on? I see that I'd recorded a couple of episodes from season seven of *Mad Men*, an episode of *The Big Bang Theory*, an episode from season three of *Homeland*, and one movie, *Kingsman: The Secret Service*. I choose the comedy, *The Big Bang Theory* – twenty-odd minutes of light-hearted nonsense.

I collect Jackie a few minutes late and we drive in relative silence to the restaurant. She seems preoccupied and I wonder whether something is wrong but choose not to ask. She'll tell me if it's something she wants to share. As for me, I'm focusing on the drive, happy to relearn alternate ways to get around.

After ordering from the menu, Jackie says, 'How was the wedding?'

'Fine. I survived. Nobody reacted adversely to the speech.'

'Did you remember anyone?'

'Only those I met days before. It was kind of bizarre, the entire experience. But the process of avoiding people I should know is taxing,' I say. I note that Jackie isn't her bubbly self.

'Did you meet old girlfriends?'

I smile. So is this her problem? 'How would I know?'

She laughs. 'So nobody came up to you inviting you to share the night with her?'

She's onto me. What do I say? Do I tell her the truth and risk ending the relationship I seem to have with her or do I lie and maintain a sense of purity? I drink some water. 'I tried to keep away from trouble.'

'Tried?'

'I had to rescue a damsel in distress.'

'This is a noisy place,' Jackie says, and I wonder whether she is changing the subject. 'Anyway I'm pleased you had a good time. I had an early night reading a book, accompanied by only a glass of white wine.'

'And some chocolate,' I add.

'Of course. Chocolate is always nice.'

We eat and chat about nothing controversial for as long as the meal takes. On the way home I finally ask whether something is wrong. I suspect she feels miffed about my comment on the wedding but I can't read her. I have to wonder whether this odd behaviour is simply Jackie's, or are all females mysterious about their thoughts and feelings.

'I've had some work problems. I received a call just after you called me and was told one of my employees was in an accident and won't be at work for weeks.'

'Oh,' I say, relieved I wasn't responsible for her contemplative mood. 'Can you get somebody in temporarily?'

'Perhaps. But Jenny is a good friend and I want her to be okay. She's in hospital. I'll see her tomorrow. Yesterday's visiting hours was for family only.'

'Car accident?'

'She fell off her bicycle going down a hill and was lucky not to have been hit by a car.'

At Jackie's place I wait to be invited in but nothing is forthcoming, so I leave with a soft but brief kiss to the lips. Obviously Jackie is distracted so it's best I simply go away. Admittedly, if I were in her shoes I'd still want to enjoy her body. I'm driving away when my iPhone buzzes. I stop and answer. It's Don Murphy.

Chapter 16 Monday

The sound of birds chirping brings my sleep to an end. I see from my digital clock that it is only six-forty. I get up full of energy. I stretch and do some push-ups and sit-ups. It's time I forget about my amnesia and carry on with my life afresh. I don't know if I exercised previously but it's a good idea and I've started today.

As I shower I recall the conversation with Murphy the night before. He wanted to meet this morning at eleven forty-five at the usual place. I refused, saying I would meet him at a restaurant bar in George Street, the one near Martin Place. He reluctantly agreed when I wouldn't change my mind. I'm sure the slimy bugger can handle meeting at a recognised eating place, rather than on some ridiculous bench in a people-infested park. After breakfast I walk down to my usual café and order a cappuccino. Julie brings it over and I ask how the weekend was.

'Not great. I broke up with my boyfriend,' she says.

'How is that possible? Is he nuts? But it does leave you available for me,' I say, grinning.

She grimaces. 'I don't think so – not with a womaniser like you.'

'Have you ever seen me with a female?'

'Often, you cad. You have them chasing after you,' she says.

'I've changed,' I say, but realise I don't have a clue about my past experiences.

Walking back home, I notice more new things. The houses, the contours of the road, trees. It's a warm day with wispy clouds up high and I'm inclined to waste time lying around my flat. But I need to read the material Murphy gave me so I can ask some tough questions. I spend some time taking notes then I hurry to the bus stop.

I arrive at the bar ten minutes early, order a beer and sit outside watching the traffic and people. Donald Murphy wanders in at eleven-fifty. He is wearing grey slacks, a white shirt and black shoes, which are not polished. He looks around and when he sees me, walks over in a slow side step, avoiding tables and other customers. As he slides into a chair opposite me, I ask whether he'd like a drink. He shakes his head. Obviously he is here to deliver a message. It seems he can't combine business with a little pleasure.

'I can't stay,' he says.

'Okay,' I say, looking at his pale face, his wrinkles and his unruly thin hair. He reminds me of a little old man complaining about everything in life, although he wouldn't be more than sixty. I add, 'You wanted to meet, as I recall.'

'I did. I hope you will be sensible with the story.' Murphy looks around furtively. Does he expect to be shot or something?

'I will,' I say, waiting for more.

His eyes are studying me. I've never seen him smile or show any signs of happiness but I guess his aim is to leak stuff that is unpleasant. He says, 'I think, if possible, you should avoid any reference to Mr Antonovich.'

I wait. I want him to squirm. I don't know why exactly but suddenly I see the whole business as slimy. I'm expected to muddy the character of an Australian MP but not mention other parties who are also potentially guilty of corruption. Finally, after taking another mouthful of beer, I ask, 'Why?'

'Well Mr Antonovich might sue,' he says.

'What about the minister?'

Murphy looks like a cornered rat. 'Not likely,' he finally says.

'Let me ask you this. How did you come by this information?'

Murphy flicks a stray thin hair off his face. 'I can't tell you that.'

'How do I know it's true, then?' I stare at him, hoping he's going to either level with me or feel uncomfortable. I don't like this man and can't imagine why I trusted him.

'You had no problem with this before. I can take it to another journalist. Is that what you want?'

I ignore the statement. 'I've done some reading in the last few days. In your notes you don't say which Minister for Defence it is. There's been a change of portfolios so is it the current one or the former?'

Murphy looks like a sad little man and I fear he might burst into tears. He gets up the courage to raise his head. 'The former one, of course. Look, I have to get going.'

I realise I won't get much more out of Murphy so I don't object. I may need him again. 'All right. Can you tell me where I can get you at work?'

He looks bemused. 'You can't talk to me at work.'

'If you want Antonovich's name to be missing from my article, you need to be more co-operative,' I say, knowing I have some leverage.

He asks for my iPhone and taps a number under his name. He leaves without further ado. He's a strange individual, given he wants this piece to be written. He's obviously not in customer service.

I wait at Martin Place train station, wanting to experience different forms of travel. When the train arrives I wander into a carriage and take the stairs to the top deck, sit down and begin flicking through the pages of a newspaper I'd bought. After a while I look up and see a woman staring at me. When she sees I'm looking at her she smiles. How odd. I return to the paper. At Edgecliff station I look up again and notice that the olive skinned, dark-haired woman is doing something on her phone. Good. Maybe I was a curiosity or someone who reminded her of a cousin or long-forgotten friend. I mean if she actually knew me she'd make her way to sit next to me. Unless she expected me to move to her. It's all too much. I continue reading an article on cricket.

The train stops at Bondi Junction, the last stop. Everybody still on the train gets up and waits for the doors to open. The woman who had smiled at me is suddenly next to me.

'Hello, Nick,' she says.

My God, I think. She does know me and I don't know how to react. Was she a girlfriend or a work colleague or is she a relative? 'Hi, what are you doing here on a work day?' I hope I sound convincing and that she isn't a stay-at-home mum or something.

'You're joking. You've always been a joker. Don't you remember me? I'm Lauren O'Keefe from the bank. You came in to the branch six months ago to arrange an investment mortgage.'

'Of course I remember,' I lie. Relief floods through me. So I haven't slept with her and she's not a cousin or an aunt, although she'd be in her thirties, a bit young for an aunt. But she is attractive so sleeping with her wouldn't be out of the question.

We walk out of the train and together follow the crowd out of the station. 'How are you these days? Is the rented property giving you any trouble?'

'No, it's good,' I say, playing along. So I'm a landlord. Wow. Which makes me wonder how I made enough money to invest in property. Did I do some super paying jobs or rob a bank? I almost laugh out loud.

'I had to pop into Head Office this morning,' Lauren reveals, 'but I have time for a drink, if you fancy one?'

'Sounds good but I need to take care of a few things first. I'll walk you to your branch because I need to get some information.'

'Great. That'll give me time to freshen up a bit too. Do you need another loan?'

'No,' I say wondering how this is going to play out. 'Just some basic information one of your colleagues can help with.'

We arrive at the branch, which is inside the Westfield complex. Lauren asks one of her colleagues to look after me and says she'll see me in ten minutes.

I am shown to a little office. A young woman with a nametag that indicates she's called Kelly offers me coffee or tea. I decline the drinks and wonder why I'm given such treatment. She asks how she can help, a lovely smile lighting up her face.

'I've had trouble with my computer,' I say. 'I just want a run-down on the balances I have with the bank. And I was hoping you could help me reset my password.'

She coughs, places a hand over her mouth, and looks at me. 'That's no problem at all.'

After a moment's work on the computer that she has in front of her, she says, 'Usually we'd need to ask for photo ID for such a request but we know you and Lauren is sweet on you so I'll just write it down on this piece of paper. I'll also give you a temporary password which you'll need to change when you get home.'

'Absolutely,' I say. I feel like I'm getting my life back together. All I have to do is get to my medical appointment later in the afternoon.

Kelly leaves, giving me an opportunity to examine the data she has collected. I see that I have a mortgage on a property in Glebe for $600,000. I also have a cheque account for $12,345, a cash management account of $126,450, a fixed term deposit of $300,000, and a share account worth over six million dollars.

Then Lauren pops in. 'Ready?' she asks.

'Yes,' I say. I hope she can throw some light on my financial situation.

Chapter 17 Monday

Lauren is sitting opposite me in a wine bar and I ask how she has the time to socialise. It seems that while Kelly was attending to me, Lauren had touched up her make-up and hair. She wears her short hair layered but piled high and away to the right, accentuating the oval shape of her face.

'You're funny, Nick! You're an important client and I'm working. Although I must admit this is very pleasant work – mingling with a wealthy and handsome individual. The bank is happy for me to spend as much time as I want. We don't want to lose you, Nick.'

'Right,' I say. How did I accrue this wealth? I'm in my early thirties and there are only two ways for anyone as young as I am to be as rich as I appear to be. From inheritance or as a major drug dealer. I'm almost afraid to find out but I sip my wine and enjoy the attention. 'You don't have to worry, I have no intention of doing anything radical.'

'That's something else I love about you, you're so modest. Nick, why don't you quit your journalist job and write full time as you've said you'd do when I talked with you previously? You can certainly afford it … unless you love being a journalist.'

'I'm just finishing off a job. Then I'll consider my options.' Writing a book; did I really voice this ambition?

'Would you consider inventing another phone app? I guess that's easier said than done.'

'I doubt it. I wouldn't know where to start.'

Lauren touches my arm. 'You're gifted. Just admit it. You could be a full time investor, a writer or an inventor. You have everything anyone could wish for, although I know nothing about your relationships.'

Nor do I, I was about to say but I stay silent. To avoid the topic I say, 'Do you use my app?'

'Of course not. You sold it to Apple and they'll release it next year, according to what you said a month ago. You're odd today, is everything all right?' Lauren says looking at me strangely.

I glance at my watch. Then I say, 'I have an appointment so I'll have to get going but thanks for the drink.'

'Any time, Nick. Be good.'

Outside, I catch a taxi. Being rich can change you. Why would I get public transport? Daft. I arrive at the Carrington Street Development Clinic a few minutes before my appointment. I have my brain scanned for obvious signs of physical damage and I'm told to report to the doctor who referred me the following week. This process will determine whether my condition is as a result of physical or other trauma.

On the way back I stop at Jackie's flat. I'm not sure why but I want to ask how her day with her staff problems turned out. When I'm at the front door I hear talking.

'I can't,' Jackie says.

'You mean you don't want to,' a male voice says.

'Look …' It's Jackie again. I knock on the door. If nothing else, it may end the argument.

Jackie opens the door. 'Hi,' she says. 'Come in.'

I follow Jackie in and confront a tall, thin man who is unshaven and possesses wild eyes. I suspect he might be on drugs and wonder what the hell he is doing here. If he's threatening Jackie, I'll break him in two. Jackie introduces him as Josh and tells him I'm a friend.

Before Josh can say anything another woman appears. She is short and also thin and has unruly straw-coloured hair. 'What's the shouting about?'

Josh says, 'Jackie won't come to the jazz.'

'Maggie, this is my friend Nick.'

I shake Maggie's extended hand. Josh, still caught up with himself, doesn't bother with the handshaking. He appears put out by my arrival.

Maggie turns to Jackie. 'Why won't you come?'

'I'm tired and I'm not that interested in the scene.'

'Your friend can come along,' Maggie says.

'Sorry, I'm taking Jackie to dinner,' I say.

Maggie looks at Jackie. 'You should have said.'

'She forgot our date,' I say. 'It's not her fault.'

Josh and Maggie look at each other. 'Okay,' says Maggie. 'We've got to go.' The two kiss Jackie on the cheek and leave.

'Thanks,' Jackie says. 'They're persistent and I didn't know how to get out of it. Josh usually won't take no for an answer.'

'Who are they?'

'Uni friends. They love jazz and hip-hop and I don't. Thanks again.'

'Would you like to go out to dinner? My treat.'

'That's kind of you but I've had a big day.'

I move closer and hold her hands in mine. 'If you really need time alone, that's fine but I've got some good news and I want to celebrate.'

'You have other women to ask out, don't you?'

I see apprehension in her eyes. 'Who?'

'I saw you today at Westfield. You were with a well-dressed attractive woman.'

I laugh. 'I see. That was my bank liaison officer.'

Her lips break out into a smile. 'I wondered why you didn't pop into the salon.'

'I also had a medical appointment otherwise I would have.'

We agree to go to a local restaurant in Bondi. We chat and I learn that Jackie is undertaking a part-time university course. She's into the third year and met Josh and Maggie a year ago. It seems she can have one of her staff manage the business while she goes in for lectures. She asks about my medical appointment and is pleased to hear I'm doing positive things for my condition.

'So what are we celebrating?' she asks when the coffee arrives.

'The fact that I'm not poor. In fact, according to the bank information I checked out, I'm able to eat for some weeks to come.'

'Meaning what?'

'It seems I invented something that made me a decent amount of money. I don't know the details or the full extent of my wealth but let's say I'm financially okay.'

'That's good news. So it's really important that you establish who you are.'

'I guess. But right now I want to savour the moment.' Although it appears that I'm fortunate, I may be in for disappointment when I finally wake up and find out who I am, not in name but in essence. Life seems to be a fragile thing. The more I read or listen to the news the gloomier the world appears.

Jackie says, 'That's good. I hope when you do reappear as the real Nick and not a stranger, you'll still have me as a friend.'

'How can you doubt that?'

'Stranger things have happened.'

'Very funny,' I say.

We finish up and I drive Jackie back home. Outside the flat, she says, 'I'm not going to invite you in. I think we should cool it until you get your memory back.'

'Why?'

'I'm starting to really like you. In fact I think I'm falling for you, but I've been disappointed so many times so I'd rather ...'

'Do you think I'll abandon you once my memory returns?'

Jackie places her hand over mine. 'I hope not but you'll soon get back to your normal life and the people in it.'

'Perhaps, but what do you think might happen? That a wife or lover will emerge?'

'It's possible. But let's wait.'

I agree reluctantly. As I drive off I realise that I need to find out about my parents.

Chapter 18 Tuesday

The new day pulsates with energy. I stumble out of bed, yawning. Remembering my vow to get fit, I go through a routine of strength and aerobic exercises. Then breakfast before I begin the first assignment for the day.

I'd been through my iPhone contact list but hadn't found anyone with the surname "Hunter", let alone names such as "Mum", "Dad" or "Home". I try again, studying each name from the As through to the Zs. Nothing. Am I an orphan or adopted? Did I change my name?

Then a thought occurs to me as I look over Rose Bay towards the water. I rifle through my emails. It seems I've put some into folders and have kept only messages from the last month. None of the current emails helps me. I review the folders and find one called "Personal". I open this folder and after checking out a variety of messages, I come across one headed "Holiday". I open it and find the author is someone called Sally McIntyre.

In the email, Sally explains that she's gone on a tour of China and that she won't be able to reach me for some weeks. It's dated four days before my amnesia and signed "Mum". So I have a mother but my father is still a mystery. I'll wait for her return then ask the many questions for which I need answers. I note that my contact list includes the name Sally McIntyre. This is also odd. Maybe she isn't really my mother and I am adopted. Who knows?

That settled, I sit down in front of my computer and continue writing my article. I base it on my original draft together with the additional information Murphy gave me. I also research certain aspects online. Time goes by quickly as I became immersed in the story. I forget to eat lunch and when I next look at the time it's after 3 pm. I go to the fridge and then the phone interrupts my decision on what to eat. It's Dr Birnstein, the specialist, and he tells me that he has some news. He wants me to meet him as soon as I'm able to. I say I'll drop in later today.

On the journey to see Dr Birnstein I worry about this meeting. It must be bad news. I was told the results would be available next week. So it's been rushed. Perhaps I have only got a few short weeks left to live? I imagine what I might do during my last days. Go on a holiday to Europe or America or around the world? Make love to as many women as possible? Commit suicide? The options are endless.

In the doctor's office, I'm sitting on a chair facing an empty desk. The doc walks in after letting me hang for five minutes and, when he finally sees me, he smiles. Is he a sadist? Why not simply tell me the grim news?

'Well, I have some good news and some bad news,' he says.

I wish he'd just get on with it and not pussyfoot around. Just tell me the number of months or days I have left. I don't have time to waste.

When I don't respond, he continues. 'The scans show that you have no physical injury.' He looks at me. 'You have psychological trauma.'

I regard Dr Birnstein for a moment. Is he pulling my chain? 'Are you sure?'

'Absolutely. What you have is psychogenic amnesia, which is a condition characterised by abnormal memory functioning. This condition results from severe stress or psychological trauma, like Repressed Memory Syndrome.'

'I see,' I say, totally mystified. 'And is it something that can be cured?'

'It usually resolves itself in time. But how long is something that can't be predicted.'

'What would have caused it?'

Dr Birnstein glances out the window for a moment, then turns back. 'It's most commonly associated with traumatic events or violent experiences involving emotional shock, such as being mugged or raped or involved in a car crash.'

'What about an attack in a bar?'

'Possibly. Only you will be able to confirm that when your memory returns. Unless, of course, whatever brought it on is blocked by your mind.'

I push my hand through my hair and note that it needs a cut. 'Why would it be blocked?'

'Sometimes the event is so traumatic that the mind can't face it. But the mind is an unusual mechanism that is still not fully understood.'

'Is there anything which could hurry the process?' I ask.

'Just go about your day-to-day activities as you would and don't try too hard to remember. It's likely the event which caused the memory loss will come back to you if you just relax and let the mind do its thing.'

After some more informal chat, I shake Dr Birnstein's hand and leave. I catch a taxi to Bondi Junction and go to Jackie's salon for a haircut. I walk along level one of the Westfield Mall and wait outside the salon to assess how busy it is. I'm in luck. Only one customer. As I enter the sleek establishment, the receptionist asks me how she can help. 'I just need a trim,' I say.

I'm seated and I wonder where Jackie is, as I haven't spotted her yet. Then, once I'm ready to be attended to, she pops out of a back office. At first she seems stunned by my appearance, then she walks up and tells her colleague that she'll look after me.

'What are you doing here?' she enquires.

'I'm after a haircut,' I say, peering at her via the mirror.

She gathers her implements and lets me wait until everything she needs is prepared. 'Okay. What did you have in mind?' She looks unusually busty with her tight blue top and she's ready to do damage with legs astride. I feel something stir below my belt but focus on her face.

'What do you recommend to make me appear professional?'

'So you want to be in my hands?'

'Absolutely,' I say, settling in for a surprise haircut.

As she works on me I enjoy her touch, closing my eyes to get the full benefit of her skilful hands. I imagine her as an Amazon princess who is in charge of my body. She doesn't talk. Small talk would be wasted and having just broken up, she may want to keep quiet about that as well. But I can enjoy the moment.

As she brushes off loose hair from my scalp I say, 'I saw the specialist earlier and he told me my amnesia is not the result of physical injury.'

'Oh,' she says. 'What does that mean?'

'It means the blow to the head wasn't the cause of my mind snap. It must be something else. Like seeing something at the same time I was attacked that freaked me out.'

'What could you have seen?' Jackie removes the barber's sheet from me.

'That's what you may know because you were there and your memory's intact. Can you recall who was in the pub at the time of the assault?'

Jackie looks puzzled. I stand and face her. She says, 'Not off the top of my head but let me think about it. Give me a few hours.'

'Okay,' I say. 'Good job with the haircut.'

'Thanks. It makes you look even more handsome.'

I'm taken aback. I can't figure whether she wants to resume our relationship or not. 'So when you've thought about that night, would you call or email or even invite me over for a drink?'

'We'll see,' she says going to the cash register, 'That's twenty-five dollars, special rate for a special customer.'

'Thanks,' I say. I pay in cash and walk out of the salon.

Later that night I get a call from Jackie. 'I've been thinking and I'd like to help but I'm not sure I can,' she says.

My heart sinks. I can see myself being in a state of limbo for who knows how long. Dr Birnstein didn't say my memory would return,

100

simply that it might and that the timing was unpredictable. 'I see,' I say.

'But if you'd like to come over, I'll fill you in on what I can recall.'

'When?'

'Now would be fine, unless you are in the middle of something.'

I find it hard to contain my enthusiasm. 'I'll be there soon.'

For somebody with money, I'm surprised that I have no wine cellar. All I found as I studied my flat in the last few days was a small wine rack containing a dozen bottles, mainly reds but some whites. I grab a Wolf Blass Sauvignon Blanc Semillon trusting that Jackie will enjoy it. Then as I'm driving I realise white wine should be cold and this bottle isn't. Am I going nutty as well as having lost my memory?

But when I hand the bottle to Jackie she shows appreciation and kisses my cheek. As much as I want to kiss her, I resist and follow her into the flat. She invites me to sit and asks whether I'd like a coffee. I decline. Then she begins her story. 'I remember you at the bar. You were standing next to a tall man in slacks and a striped blue shirt. You seem to be looking into the mirror when the other man enters, the one who strikes you.'

'Okay, so I'm oblivious to the guy who hits me?'

'Apparently. You seem to be transfixed by something. Perhaps what you see in the mirror.'

'Thanks. It doesn't clear anything up though.'

Jackie stands then moves towards the refrigerator and takes out a bottle of white wine. 'Would you like some?'

'Sure,' I say. I'm sure she noted the dejection in my voice.

She places a glass of wine in front of me and sits opposite. 'I've just had a thought. Maybe Charmaine or Max, who were facing the door, can recall who else was in your vision.'

'Would you ask them?'

'Of course. There's another reason I asked you to pop over.' Jackie looks down at her glass.

'There is?' I'm intrigued.

'I've been thinking. I have been unpleasant to you for no reason. It's not your fault you lost your memory, and ...'

'Does this mean you're okay with still seeing me?'

'Sure, but let's take it slow.'

I raise my hands in a defensive gesture. 'Absolutely.' I feel buoyed, exuberant, high. I stand and she does too and we kiss. Then she holds me back and says she needs to make some calls but asks me to wait. Then she gives me an address.

I leave, trusting that Charmaine can add something useful.

Chapter 19 Tuesday

Charmaine is a squirrelly-looking woman. Long nose and forward-pushing jaw with crazy brown hair that seems out of control. But she greets me enthusiastically. Shakes my hand, asks me to sit down. Offers a beer, which I accept. I need something. As she tends to the drinks she calls out, saying she lives by herself and that Max is simply a friend, not somebody with whom she has a relationship. And then she tells me she went to school with Jackie and that they're close friends. Finally the beer comes, courtesy of her fridge, and she faces me. In a sense I'm pleased we are sitting and drinking. She has a white wine in front of her, on a coaster, on the table between us. I was afraid she'd tell me her whole life story but now she focuses on me.

'Jackie says you need me to recall what happened the night we met you,' she says.

'Yes, that would be good if you could tell me what you saw.' I don't know how much Jackie has told her so I tread lightly.

'That's right, you were knocked out so you can't remember much from that evening?'

'Correct. I'm in the dark. Can you help?'

Charmaine strokes her chin between two fingers. 'Let me see. I was next to Max and across from Jackie. Two guys entered as I recall but I'm not sure that they were together because the second man turned and left soon after the first guy walked up to you.'

'So you saw both men clearly?'

'Not really. Jackie saw the fellow who hit you because she was looking in that direction. As I recall you were walking away from the bar with a drink when you were hit on the side of your head. I was looking at the door and wondered why the man walked out again after looking at the people in front of him. He seemed to be staring at something but I've no idea what.'

'Okay. What did he look like?' I'm getting impatient and I hope like hell she remembers.

'He was a stocky fellow with these big black framed glasses. Can't remember much else.'

Charmaine sips her drink. 'Does that help?'

I scratch my head. 'Can't say it does. But thanks anyway.'

We finish our drinks. Charmaine, the chatty person she is, tells me how she became Jackie's friend in high school. Apparently, Charmaine was not in any group at school and felt isolated, sometimes bullied, until Jackie invited her to join the group she hung around with. From then on Charmaine remained loyal to Jackie throughout her school years and beyond.

Finally I stand, thank Charmaine again and head for the door.

Charmaine sees me out then at the door says, 'I just remembered. The guy with the glasses had a bushy moustache too.'

For the briefest of moments something flashes through my mind. But whatever it was, it disappears too quickly to reveal itself.

At home I check the time. It's late but I need to take my mind off my situation so I grab a novel and go to bed. I don't know what I usually read, but the book that had been lying on the table next to the sofa was probably the one I had lined up. It's a Lee Child crime novel, which I don't seem to have started.

Hands encircle my throat from behind. The hands are powerful and I feel my life draining from me. Using my right elbow I thrust it backwards and sense it smash into flesh. The hands disappear. I turn and see my assailant. He is a strong looking man with black-rimmed glasses and a brown moustache. I wake, sweating. The nightmare seemed so real. I get up and walk into the bathroom. I splash water on my face and look in the mirror. Who was that guy? I don't know but I sense that I should.

It's 4:12 am. And I can't sleep. I take my laptop and return to bed. I research Australian Defence Ministers. I find it hard to believe the material Murphy has provided. Something isn't right.

After a few hours work I get up and shower. I know what my next step will be.

Chapter 20 Wednesday

As I enjoy a coffee and a breakfast of pancakes and strawberries at my usual café, I ponder the information I gleaned. Julie comes over to my table and asks if everything is all right.

'Everything's fine except for one thing,' I say looking up at a serious face.

'Oh, what's that?'

'You have a lovely smile and you need to do it more.'

'Well, I'm not too happy at the moment,' Julie says.

'Why's that? The sun is out, the birds are chirping. What could be wrong with the world?' Of course she doesn't know the problems I face – amnesia, a story about corruption I've half written which sounds unbelievable, and a lady friend who seems to run hot and cold.

'You know, I told you my boyfriend and I broke up over the weekend.'

I peer at her, seeing the pain in her eyes. 'It's not good,' I say, 'but you're young and pretty and you'll soon meet another guy.'

'Are you trying to cheer me up?' She finally smiles.

'Just telling it the way I see it. Do you want him back?'

Julie looks around to see whether she is needed then turns back to me and says, 'No, I wouldn't have him back. I discovered he painted pictures, which he copied then tried to flog as originals. But that's not all. He's lied to me about a number of things.'

'Oh,' I say, taking a sip of coffee. 'Was he seeing someone else?'

'I think so. Anyway, whatever he does or says, nothing's authentic. I'm just over him. I have to get back to work.' Julie moves quietly to the counter to pick up another order that's ready to go.

I watch as she goes about her work and wonder whether the experience with her boyfriend has left her scarred. Will she find men hard to trust in future? Or is she one of those positive people not troubled by minor setbacks? I suspect I'm not the trusting kind but have to find out more about myself before I can draw that kind of conclusion. It seems weird to think I don't know the person I am. Very odd.

On my walk up the slope to my flat I think about the word "authentic". And I wonder whether the material I received from Don Murphy is authentic. At home I realise that I'd forgotten my mobile phone. I pick it up and see there's a message. I listen. A female voice says: 'Hello darling, I'm back. We had an awesome time. Sorry I didn't call but the place was too remote to get a signal. Call me. I can't wait to see you again.'

Who is this? I check the details and the name that crops up is Claire Harper. Do I have a girlfriend? Another female in my life? I won't call her now, the surprise is too much for me at this point, but I may do it later. Instead I focus on the material I have and examine it closely. One comment strikes me as odd. I research articles online and come across one entitled: "Uranium on offer to Islamic State". It talks about criminal networks with suspected Russian ties seeking to sell bomb-grade material to the Middle East. But it turns out that the client was a plant and the Russian was arrested.

I can't figure exactly how this might relate to an Australian Member of Parliament dealing with a Russian representing a Middle Eastern buyer. There is a similarity but the purpose of the other piece was to highlight the sting, which resulted in an arrest. If I wrote about an activity involving a prominent Australian politician over arms deals, it would cause undue fear if it were untrue. I have to verify the data. I get up, stretch and walk to the fridge to check what I have for lunch. Nothing appeals. I feel restless because I can't decide how to proceed. I want to see Jackie but I also need to resolve the Claire mystery. As well as check all the facts in the Don Murphy files.

Outside it is warm and the sky is partially blue. White clouds float across the heavens and I wonder whether they will become dark before long, matching my increasingly changing and gloomy mood. I take my car and drive to Bondi Junction and park in the Westfield complex. I go to a café and order a coffee. I wonder whether I should pop in to see Jackie but also realise my constant appearance might spook her. I need to think. How do I confirm the details contained in the files I've been given? Obviously Murphy and Antonovich aren't going to help. Should I contact the Defence Minister's staff? What would they say? They'd deny any wrongdoing, wouldn't they?

Contemplating all this, I am ambushed by someone who has snuck up behind me.

'Hello stranger,' she says.

I turn to see Jackie and my heart lightens. 'Hi.'

'You look like you have the weight of the world on your shoulders.'

I smile. 'Join me for some lunch.'

Jackie sits across from me and examines a menu. 'I'm famished.'

'You look beautiful. I love your dress, flatters your curves.'

'Thanks. So can you tell me what's bothering you?' She puts the menu aside.

'This piece of writing is giving me problems. And I've had a message from another person who knows me. This memory loss is becoming a real bother.'

'Who is this person?'

'I don't know except that her name is Claire and she's come back from somewhere.'

'Another girlfriend or wife perhaps?'

The waiter hovers over us. We order. Then I wonder whether it was wise to reveal this information. I can sense that Jackie feels uneasy. I say, 'I'll have to face it but it doesn't mean anything. As far as I'm concerned you're my girlfriend.'

'Really,' she says. 'When have I agreed to be your girlfriend?'

This remark surprises me. Is she playing games or have I lost perspective of how females work? 'Sorry, I guess it is presumptuous of me.'

'Just sort out your women issues before you and I become a couple. Okay?'

'Sure,' I say, wanting to disappear into the ground.

We eat and when Jackie stands to leave she says she will pay and she completely ignores my protestations.

On my way home I ponder the pros and cons of full disclosure. Surely, as a journalist I would be able, at least I would once have been able, to create credible stories. It seems whatever ability I had in the lying department has deserted me.

It's mid-afternoon and I need to deal with a potentially important matter. With scotch and water in hand, I sit at the kitchen table. I take a drink then set the tumbler down. After pressing recent calls on my iPhone, I hit "Claire".

Chapter 21 Wednesday

The phone buzzes for a while and just when I'm about to give up, a voice answers, 'Hello, darling. How are you?'

I'm not sure how I should address her. Did I have a special endearment for her? So I play it safe. 'I'm okay, Claire. How was the trip?'

'Great. How have you been?'

'Can't complain,' I say, not wanting to complain. 'What part of your trip did you enjoy the most?' I want to focus on her, not me.

'Let's get together and I'll tell you all about it. I have some great photos of Chile and Argentina.'

'Where shall we meet?' I say, realising I have to face her. I wonder if I should tell her about my amnesia. But first I'd better meet Claire and judge whether it's a wise move. I've already misjudged Jackie. Yet Claire may be used to me and might be totally understanding.

'I'm unpacking and the place is a mess. How about getting together at The Anchor?'

'Okay, see you at 6:30 this evening.'

So that's why I happened to be at The Anchor that Saturday night. Is it our usual meeting place, and did I pop in that particular night to meet someone or simply because it was my regular drinking place? I look at the time and begin to get ready. This encounter will be interesting, as I don't know what she looks like. Which of the women on my iPhone photos is Claire? But as I can only guess, I better get there early to avoid any embarrassment.

I sit on a bar stool facing the array of drinks on display with a Heineken in front of me. The place is already buzzing with patrons. I book a table so that there is a spot for us when Claire arrives. I sip my beer and wait. My mind is whirling with questions. About how to handle the meeting and how to discover more about her and myself without revealing what a fraud I am. I guess I could just tell her I can't remember her but she might think it's an excuse to break up. A tap on my shoulder brings me back to the present. I turn to see a smiling face. She kisses me before I can examine her. The kiss is long and passionate. When she disengages she pulls up a stool next to me and takes my hand in hers. The bartender looks at her and she asks for a Chardonnay.

'It's so nice to see you again,' she says, 'I've missed you these past three weeks. So how are you?'

'Work has occupied my days, leaving not much time for anything else,' I say. 'I've booked a table,' I add, to ensure that I don't need to elaborate.

'You're sweet. You remembered our anniversary.'

'Did I?' I'm more surprised than ever.

'Three months today. Didn't think you'd remember.'

'My memory's been playing up, I have to admit.'

The activity is increasing and the noise is rising so Claire pulls out her camera and starts showing me photos of her excursion. I take the opportunity to look at her more closely. She is buxom with shoulder-length black hair and a Roman nose. Olive skin. She wears a dark blue top, which stretches over her breasts and flows down over her black slacks. A wide black leather belt completes the ensemble. I focus again on the photos, saying little and occasionally murmuring approvingly.

We take our seats at a table and order meals and a bottle of red wine. I want her to do most of the talking as I feel I may mess up if I talk too much. So I gaze at her to get a sense of the woman I fell for in my previous consciousness. I have to admit she looks attractive and possesses a gracious smile.

'My parents loved the trip too although James wasn't too fussed. He missed his friends and was quite frustrated when he couldn't make contact.'

'Yeah, I guess three weeks away can be a bitch if the communications are down.' I hope this statement appears appropriate.

Wine is brought over, tasted by me and then poured by a young waiter. Claire thanks him and we raise glasses and toast the occasion.

'The holiday was rugged. I don't know why I agreed to travel with my parents and brother but then it was organised before I met you so I guess I had to put up with it, money being paid and all.'

'Why was it rugged?'

'All the hiking in mountainous country. But we got some great photos and we did come across some delightful villages. Dad's a keen walker and Mum loves geography.'

Our entrée arrives. We eat this in relative silence then Claire excuses herself to go to the bathroom. She's left her phone on the table. I continue flicking through her photos. I wonder what photos I may have appeared in and whether I know her parents. I run through the South American pictures and then there are photos of people. I see a photo of Claire and me eating ice cream. Then Claire and another man who might be her brother. Then I freeze. Something flashes through my mind.

'What's wrong?' Claire is back. 'You look like you've seen a ghost.'

I look up and hand the phone to Claire. 'Who's the man in the photo, the one with the moustache and thick black-framed glasses?'

'Have you been rifling through my phone?' She sounds indignant.

I have to tread carefully but I also need to find out about the man with glasses. 'Sorry, I was curious about some of the South American photos. But the guy … who is he?'

Claire's expression tells a story. Disbelief. Confusion. She peers at the photo, having gone back to it, and then holds it in front of my eyes. 'Are you pulling my leg? That's Leo with James.' She continues to stare at me to determine whether I'm playing the fool.

'I know,' I lie. 'In that picture he looks a little different I think.'

'Are you okay? You're acting a little odd, a little distant. You used to be all over me. Are you seeing someone else?'

The main course's arrival saves me from answering straight away. I wonder whether I should reveal my condition and also confess that I have found another woman. But that would be unfair to Claire, as I can't recall how close we were in our relationship. So I try something else. 'Your veal looks nice.'

'Yes, it does. Your steak looks okay too,' she says, taking one of the chips on my plate.

I don't respond, hoping she's forgotten about the question of a new woman.

'So you haven't been in touch with Leo lately?' she says.

'No.' I have some of the wine, a pleasant Pinot Noir.

'I knew you two had fallen out but I didn't know you'd both harbour such an intense grudge.'

'What can I say?' I say, knowing I have no clue why Leo, the man with the moustache, causes my mind to freak.

'It is what it is, I suppose.' Claire digs into her meal.

'How do you like Leo?'

After finishing a mouthful of salad, Claire seems distracted by a couple brushing past her. Then she returns her attention to me. 'I don't know Leo well enough to comment. I met him when James introduced me at The Anchor once. I think you were away that night, on some job.'

'What did you make of him?'

Claire pushed her fork around. 'I thought his social skills weren't great but that could be because he didn't know me.'

'Bit of a weirdo?' I say, not exactly sure what this would elicit.

'You must know him well. Just like James does.'

I wonder what she means, so I say, 'Not that well.'

'But Leo and you designed a phone app, which brought both of you sizeable riches. Didn't you work closely with him on that?'

'Yes, but I never got to really know him. He's a very elusive guy if you know what I mean.'

Claire looks up as a woman passes and says hello. Claire smiles then turns back to me. 'That was Avril. We've only met a couple of times but I know lots about her. But back to Leo. I don't understand it.'

'What don't you understand?'

'Well as you, James and Leo went to uni together it's rather odd that you say you don't really know him.'

'Sure it is but you girls talk all the time, don't you?'

'Of course. You guys don't talk about yourselves when you're together, just sport and weather, I imagine. James is the same.' Claire laughs.

'Just my point,' I say, relieved that my lack of knowledge seems plausible.

'Still I would have thought you'd be able to sort out any disagreement with Leo, as you do have a history with him,' Claire says.

'Let's not spoil the evening by talking about Leo.'

We continue chatting about other topics, none of which puts me on the spot. I pay the bill and walk out of The Anchor with Claire hanging onto my arm.

'How did you get here?' I ask.

'I walked, silly. So do you want to give me a lift home?'

My mind races. I don't know where Claire lives but I'm expected to know. 'Why don't you come over to my place?' I suggest, simply to buy time.

'Okay,' she says.

I lead her to my car not knowing how to tackle this matter. It would be so much easier to come clean. Something holds me back and I cannot fully comprehend my reluctance. Surely she'd be sympathetic if I admitted what had happened to me. So we walk and I let her get into the passenger side and close her door. She seems surprised. Don't I do this normally?

I turn the volume of the radio up so that talking is awkward. I need a plan. I focus on the road. The traffic annoys me. Everything annoys me. It seems something is stalling my mind from remembering. If this persists I'm going to have to live differently. After the visit to the specialist I'd hoped the revival would come more easily.

We arrive at my place. Claire seems familiar, just as Linda had. How many women did I have come around? It's unsettling. I hope I wasn't some kind of playboy. When my memory returns, will I revert to old habits? I offer Claire a drink.

'A white wine would be nice,' she says.

I bring her a wine and I take a beer to the sofa. My life is a mess but at least Jackie and Claire like me. It could be worse. It would be good to understand who my enemies are too.

'Why don't we move into the bedroom?' Claire says.

Decision time.

Chapter 22: Thursday

She is atop me with her large breasts pressed against my face. I'm smothered with flesh but I like it. If I have to die, and I will one day, I'd like this to be the method. But the survival instinct kicks in and I manage to get air as my mouth tackles her left breast. I hadn't thought of any reason why I shouldn't make love to Claire who, after all, is my girlfriend. So why not go with the flow? Because of my memory loss, this seems like a first-time experience and one that, I have to admit, is thoroughly enjoyable. Maybe I'll rot in hell for being so weak but that's a long way off. Besides, I don't think I believe in anything that conjures up a hell. I guess I'll know what I used to believe once my memory returns. But at the moment I'm taking this boob torture like a man.

'Oh Nick, I've missed you so much,' she says, making me once again suffocate under her as she presses her enormous orbs into my face.

I can't respond but I don't really want to alter the mood by talking. Then a phone buzzes. It's not mine because I'd switched off my mobile once we reached home.

My arms encircle her waist and as she tries to move I prevent her escape. Let the caller try again at a more convenient time. But she struggles and I realise it's a losing battle.

Claire gets off me and searches for her Samsung Galaxy phone. 'Hello,' she says after she finds it. She listens, then turns to me, distraught. 'Sorry, I have to go. Dad's in hospital with a stroke. Can you call me a taxi while I dress?'

I'm in a state of acute arousal but I do as requested. I watch as Claire gets dressed, wondering whether I'm cursed. The whole episode is somewhat surreal. When she's gone I fix myself a scotch then go to bed, to sleep.

I wake with a mighty thirst. I'm also perspiring heavily and a vision of the man with the moustache is still with me. The image haunts me even when I'm awake. I'd obviously had a nightmare. A memory of sorts comes back. Again it's a memory starring the man with the black glasses and bushy moustache. He is definitely angry, shouting some incomprehensible message. He is red with rage and I seem to be in a place I can't recognise. I get up, drink a full glass of cool water and wander back to bed. The time according to the digital clock on my bedside table is 4:15 am. Too early to stay up so I go back to bed, hoping the next dream experience will be less frightening.

At 7:35 am I awake again and I actually feel refreshed. Looking outside, I see dark clouds and I imagine it could rain. Good. I'm in the mood for rain. After breakfast I call Claire and check that her father is okay. She says he's now asleep after being observed throughout the night in intensive care, by family members. She tells me she will spend the day in bed as she's been up most of the night at the hospital, sick with worry. I ring off after telling her to get some decent rest.

I then call Don Murphy's business number.

'Hello,' a female voice answers.

'Is Don Murphy available?'

'Don hasn't been with us for a few months,' she says.

'Oh,' I say, 'what happened?'

There is a pause then she continues, 'That information is confidential. Who's calling please?'

'I'm a friend. Has Don moved to another department?'

'No, sir. He's been let go.' She hangs up.

I look at the phone. What a nerve. I have a good mind to call back and cause havoc but that would achieve little and I don't have time to waste. I have to rethink my strategy. The deadline for the article is getting closer so I need to verify the facts. No time to pussyfoot around.

I drive to Murphy's house in Redfern. As before, I park a few houses away and walk to the front, checking that nobody else is about. I open the gate and stroll to the door. I knock and wait. There is no response after another solid couple of bangs on his front door. I figure he could be out. Before going I look into the semi-detached from the front window. I glimpse something that strikes me as odd but I can't make it out.

Suddenly rain descends. It surprises me and I almost jump. I brush water off my head. I take the path to the back of the building. I walk under an awning, out of the rain. I knock on the back door then call out. Nothing. I try the door and it's not locked. I call, 'Don!' as I walk inside. Peering around I see a messy kitchen. Plates with food scum. Opened bottles, discarded milk cartons and cups on all available surfaces. Then a stench assails my nostrils. I walk through a corridor and into a lounge. I hold my nose. Don Murphy is lying on the floor, a bottle of whiskey next to him and empty pill containers strewn about. At first I freeze. Has he committed suicide or has somebody murdered him and made it appear that way? Then I realise I have a responsibility. I call the ambulance and the police but I don't leave my name.

Being careful not to leave any prints I walk into the other rooms and look for some evidence of what Don Murphy kept on the potential scandal I am to report. Using a handkerchief I find on a set of drawers, I open various dresser drawers and a desk that sits in a corner of the second bedroom. I find nothing of interest. I return to the back of the place and I'm about to leave when I decide to examine cupboards in the kitchen. Again, nothing. Then I do a really weird thing, probably as a result of watching too much crime on television. I crouch and look under the refrigerator. A flimsy leather folder lies there. I pull it out and inside there are papers. I close the folder and take it with me as I head back to my car.

On my way home I park in the Bondi Junction Westfield complex and pop in to see Jackie. When I arrive at the hairdressing salon, Jackie is attending to a customer so I sit down and read a magazine. Her assistant Emma asks whether she can help me but I say I'm waiting for

Jackie who has seen me but totally ignored me. Eventually she comes over, 'Another haircut?' she says, sarcasm heavy in her voice.

'Don't be like that,' I say, 'I'm just here to seek your opinion.'

We're sitting in a café not far from her salon, coffees in front of us, and looking at each other. I sense she wants to be with me, happy to be the person I go to for advice.

She says, 'Why do you want my view? What about the guys from your cricket team or all the women coming out of the woodwork?'

'I don't really know any of those people and I wouldn't know if I could trust them.' I touch her hand and she doesn't pull it away. 'At least you'll be honest in your view even if I don't want to hear it.'

'Okay, tell me what's on your mind.'

I remove my hand from hers and sit up straight. I tell her about what I discovered at Don Murphy's and then ask, 'Should I have stayed and talked to the police?'

'That's a tough one. However, since you've lost your memory they might not believe you had nothing to do with his death if you told them that you can't remember anything. It just sounds crazy and I don't think the cops have a sense of humour. So you probably did the right thing.'

'That's good, I'm glad you agree. I thought it might be difficult to explain. The reason for being there and so forth.' I drink some coffee and wonder whether it's the right time to explain about my meeting with Claire. But I need to sort that matter out so I have a clear conscience. The vision of her tits is still with me. 'There's something I need to talk to you about but I can't do it here, not now,' I say, wanting to give myself time to phrase my confession properly.

We chat some more about how her day has been before I say I need to get back to work. I pay and outside I peck her on the cheek before she leaves to go back to the salon.

At home I take the papers from Murphy's leather satchel and place them on the table. There are numerous pieces of paper, a dozen or more it seems. I flick through them and can't find anything of significance. The papers seem to support the material given to me. Should I read all them? At this moment I'm disinclined to do this because I can't be bothered. I open a beer and stare into space.

***

Ian is facing me at The Oaks. He has a schooner of Tooheys in front of him while I'm nursing a bottle of Peroni. Ian needed no persuading when I suggested meeting for a drink.

'How are you placed for Saturday?' he says.

'Doubt I'll be able to make it. Work.'

Ian takes a mouthful of beer then wipes a hand over the T-shirt straining against his stomach. 'Shit, we'll be two short then. Andrew and you, our best batsmen.'

'Sorry,' I say. 'Have you heard from Andrew?'

'Nah. Have you?'

'No.'

'Why would he contact us anyway? I wouldn't if I was holed up with a bird in Italy.'

'You're right. I wouldn't either.'

We drink and talk about nothing startling and I let him dominate the conversation. Finally I steer the subject to the purpose for my meeting with him, which is to find out the name of the guy who recommended me to Donald Murphy. I tell Ian that he was a tall man in a grey suit with a moustache.

Ian shakes his head. 'No idea, mate.'

'Okay, don't worry. Jasmine interrupted our conversation so I never got to the introductions,' I say.

'Oh, that bloke. I was watching the delectable Jasmine and saw her come over to you. That's Mitch Rutledge. He plays cricket against us. Don't you remember?'

'I must confess I don't.' Ian's lucky I can remember the last week or so. After asking more questions about Rutledge, I discover the name of the team he plays with and I know I can access contact details from the cricket site dedicated to our competition. I leave soon afterwards, keen to follow the trail.

At home I get a call from Claire. Damn! I have to deal with the looming issue and sort out my relationship with her. But I don't have the time right now. 'Hello,' I say.

'Nick, can you come over? I need you.'

'I've got work to do so can I take a raincheck?'

'It's late. Why do you have to work now?' Her voice is high pitched.

For a start I don't know where you live, I'm tempted to say. Besides, I do have to research stuff and call Rutledge. But I say, 'Look, as a compromise, let's have one drink at the Rose Bay Hotel. I really do have to work.'

'Then I have to drive all the way out there,' she whimpers.

'You want to see me, don't you?'

'Forget it. Can we meet tomorrow?'

'Okay. Lunch. I'll call you.'

'All right.' She hangs up.

I wonder about Claire. Was she always like this? Unreasonable? Petty? Childish? Or am I being overly sensitive? Perhaps our relationship was such that I pandered to her needs because of our physical compatibility. But I certainly don't feel like indulging her now.

I shake my head and do what needs to be done for tomorrow. Then I get some sleep. The deadline is in eighteen hours and I set the alarm for 6 am so that I can edit the article for submission should the facts be confirmed. It will be a busy day.

Chapter 23 Friday

After a few hours rewriting my piece, I call Mitch Rutledge who agrees to see me at two o'clock in the afternoon. I call Claire to suggest an earlier lunch. We agree on a time and place in Bondi Junction. She says she'll be able to do some shopping afterwards.

Sitting across from her I notice her scent. A strong perfume assails my nostrils. She's also gone to extremes with make-up and lipstick. Is she going to suggest bed after lunch, I wonder. But then I realise I don't know her. Not really. It's all new. She scans the menu. Our orders are taken and I sit back against the booth and wait.

'Nicky, what's wrong?'

'Nothing,' I say neglecting to tell her I hate being called Nicky.

'How's your father?'

'He's recovering. What timing. Had to have a stroke right when we're in the middle of something.'

'Yes, very inconvenient.' I note that she doesn't get the sarcasm.

'Even on the trip he was awkward. Mind you, so was Mother. God, sometimes I wish they wouldn't arrange family get-togethers.'

'Not keen on the folks?'

'Very funny. I've told you about how horrible they were to me growing up. Have you forgotten? It's a wonder I even agreed to go with them to South America but then I thought we'd stay at some luxury hotels instead of the treks we went on. God, never again.'

The food comes and we watch as the plates and cutlery are arranged. We taste our meals.

'Nicky, why don't we go away somewhere?' Claire slides a bare foot along my trousered leg, up until she reaches my crotch. She has eaten only a small portion of her meal, having pushed much of it around on her plate as though it's something to be played with.

'Oh, I don't know. Depends on the assignments I get.' I have no desire to go anywhere at this time.

'You don't need to worry about that, surely. You're rich.' She's looking straight into my eyes, daring me to contradict her.

'How do you know that?' I'm flabbergasted that she would bring this up.

'I know. James told me that you and Leo made a small fortune selling your app to Apple.'

'Really.'

'Yes,' she insists, 'and unlike Leo you didn't squander your money.'

'What did Leo do?' I ask, genuinely puzzled. Particularly if he seems to be the man with the dark-framed spectacles, the one who seems to have freaked me out.

'He went to Las Vegas and lost the lot. He's a gambler but you must've known that.'

'I haven't seen him in a while,' I say.

'So what do you say?' Claire persists. Is she with me because of my perceived wealth?

'About what?' I'm being deliberately obtuse.

'God Nick, aren't you paying attention? Let's go somewhere. Hawaii or Fiji.'

'Let me think about it. I've got a meeting scheduled so let's finish our lunch without quarrelling.'

'All right but we're not fighting, just talking about options,' she says.

It seems she likes to have the last word so I stay silent, focus on my pasta and then pay the bill. I walk outside with her and kiss her on the cheek. Before I can escape she grabs my face and kisses me on the lips. A moment later we part, Claire making a beeline for the shops while I hurry straight to the underground car park. In the corner of my eye, on my way through the plaza, I sense someone watching. I turn and see Jackie disappearing around a corner. Has she seen me with Claire? I pray she hasn't. But I have no time to worry about that now.

***

I find a vacant parking spot on a street near the pub, my drive over to Neutral Bay having been faster than the designated speed limits, which means I'll be lucky not to attract a fine from a camera somewhere along the route. It's five minutes after two o'clock and I'm at The Oaks waiting for Mitch Rutledge, who is also late. I ponder how to construct the conversation. Obviously not knowing why I accepted the original material means I'll have to tread carefully. I take a sip of my beer and gaze around. The place is busy with lunchtime drinkers and diners. Many of the women are accompanied by men, and most look like office workers with neat office-type clothes, dresses or skirts with suitable tops or tailored trousers and heels. A lot of the men are in suits.

My eyes are drawn to an attractive female in a yellow polka dot dress, high clunky shoes and a bun on top of her head. She has a prominent cleavage and I can imagine wrestling naked with her on a bed. But I mustn't be distracted. Then as I take another mouthful of beer, Rutledge arrives. We shake hands. I offer to buy him a drink but he waves my offer away and gets a schooner of something plus another Peroni for me. I thank him and he asks how I am.

'Great. How's the cricket going, Mitch?'

'Don't ask. Not getting many runs lately,' he says. 'I see you've scored a couple of centuries this season.'

I smile, not knowing how to respond. I'm not sure whether he's pulling my leg or not. 'I just enjoy a hit.' Then to get off the subject, I say, 'I didn't know you were such a good friend of Andrew's.'

'Yeah, we go way back. Actually played in his team some years ago. Before your time. I introduced him to Megan, if you must know.'

'I had no idea,' I say, being absolutely honest as I have little memory of anything. 'And you know Don Murphy, too. Is he a friend?'

'Didn't you hear? It was on the news. Don is dead. Suicide apparently.'

'Jesus,' I say, sounding sufficiently horrified to ensure I don't reveal I'd seen him dead. 'What reason would he have to do such a thing?'

Rutledge pulls his stool a little closer to mine and whispers, 'He lost his job and he's a guy who lived by himself with no girlfriend or boyfriend, as far as I know.'

'Is that enough to do yourself in?'

'I don't know. He had no friends as far as I knew, lonely chap really, but I didn't really know him that well. Came across him through work.'

I am intrigued. 'So how did he get you to recommend a journalist?' The woman in the yellow polka dot dress wanders past, casting an eye in my direction.

Rutledge drains his glass of beer. He's only had about three gulps and I wonder if he has a drinking problem, but to be polite I say I'll get another round. He doesn't complain so I buy him another schooner of Tooheys New. I decide to sit on my bottle of Peroni. On my return, he says, 'Don was concerned about something but he wouldn't tell me what, only that he needed to spill some damning information to the papers. We got talking and I mentioned that you were a freelance journo.'

'I see.' What he's revealed doesn't help me with my quest for verification. 'Is Murphy, I mean, was Murphy a straight shooter?'

'I don't know. But I can give you the number of someone who knew him better than I did.'

I take the number of someone called Neil Rykman. Rutledge and I finish our drinks, and he says he has to get back to the office. I call Maxine to advise her that the article won't be ready by tonight. She expresses disappointment but otherwise doesn't give me grief about it.

I arrange to meet Neil Rykman later in the evening. On the phone he tells me he used to work with Don in the same department. Before I can do anything else, Claire calls.

'Hi Nicky, are you free tonight?'

'Sorry, I'm off to interview somebody on a piece I'm doing.'

'But it's Friday night. This is crazy, you've always seen me on Fridays. Sometimes your wretched cricket interferes on Saturday night but Friday was our night.'

So she doesn't like me playing cricket on Saturday. I've got a good mind to make myself available for tomorrow. Instead I say, 'This is important unfortunately, so let's get together on Sunday, shall we?'

'I don't know. I may have other plans.'

'Well, that's bad luck.' I close the call before she can start up again. It occurs to me that I may have been a bastard in my former life but I can't be held hostage to habits I have no idea of, can I? I'm a new man, a born again man and I have to live with it.

***

Neil Rykman lives in a one-level dwelling in Rhodes. It's dark when I arrive and he opens the front door a few moments after I ring the bell. He shows me in and introduces me to his wife who says hello and then leaves. She says she has a meeting at the local church. Rykman asks me whether I'd like a drink and I agree to a scotch and dry.

'So you want to talk about Don Murphy?' he begins.

'I understand you knew him well,' I say, comfortably seated on a well-worn couch opposite Rykman, who's occupying an equally worn armchair. The living room is filled with old furniture and a television with a small screen. I get the impression that the Rykmans are careful with their funds.

'I worked with him for years but this was before he moved into the Department of Defence. So that was, let me think, nearly three years ago now.' Rykman licks his lips. He is almost bald, with a few white hairs struggling to appear around the sides of his head, and he has a round pale face.

'Did you keep in touch with him after he was transferred?'

'Oh yes, we met up every now and then. He had few real friends.'

I drink some scotch. 'What sort of person was he?'

'Negative, very negative. Never had anything good to say about anybody. I remember once he described one woman he knew as part of the dross of humanity.'

'Who was he talking about?'

'Someone's wife, I think it was the wife of his boss after he'd been to a work function.'

'So did he have a beef with anybody at the Department of Defence?'

Rykman laughs. 'He had a beef with almost everyone. He hated his job but did it because there was no alternative.'

'I see. So would he provide malicious material to harm someone's reputation?'

Rykman leans back and clasps his hands at the back of his head. 'Not of his own doing. He's a follower. Didn't have an original thought in his head but if someone put him up to it, I wouldn't be surprised if he did so. I don't think he liked people.'

'So he could be bribed?'

'I'd say so. He wasn't well off.'

'Any expensive habits – drugs, women, gambling?' I ask this innocently but I need to have a full picture of Murphy's character. The longer this interview goes on the less inclined I'm likely to take the material he's passed on to me at face value.

'He liked a drink and he bet on the horses, that's about it. I don't think he visited brothels, never talked about it anyway.'

I also need to understand why Neil Rykman talks so easily about a supposed friend. 'Were you his closest friend then?'

'I still work in the city and Don used to meet me at my regular

Friday night haunt. That's why I couldn't see you earlier because I had a few drinks at the pub with colleagues.'

'And Don joined you and your mates.'

'Yes. Usually he and I would drink together when the other public servants had gone home. He didn't show tonight.'

'Did you know he's dead?'

'I heard a rumour he'd committed suicide but I didn't believe it.'

'Why? From what you've told me he was a sad case.'

'True enough but he wouldn't have the guts to do something like that. He was a miserable sod but he seemed happy in his misery, if you know what I mean.' Rykman finished his brandy.

'Thanks for your help,' I say, standing. I leave even more confused than before. So Murphy didn't have friends, male or female, wasn't likely to take his own life, and would pass on dubious information if someone paid him to do it. What was the truth about the files leaked to me? I had more work to do.

On the drive home, I park my car outside Jackie's duplex.

Chapter 24 Friday/Saturday

Jackie lives on the top part of a duplex in Bellevue Hill. She told me that the ground level portion of the duplex was occupied by a couple of lesbians but I hadn't seen anyone from there. I sit in my car and wonder whether it's wise to simply turn up. It is 11 pm and I struggle with myself about this impulsive gesture. But I want to see her. I could phone first. Of course her phone might be turned off or she might suggest not coming around. I'll be brave. I climb the stairs and knock on her door. She might also be with somebody else, a man even.

The night is neither hot nor cold. I'm not confident. In fact, I'm prepared to be rejected.

The door opens after only a minute's wait but the time seems interminable. I smile but it's not returned. 'Hello,' I say.

'Come in,' she commands, and I wonder whether she wants to punish me with a whip.

I do as I'm told but I'm reluctant to touch her, as she appears fierce. 'I hope I'm not disturbing you.'

'You are,' she says, 'I have a lover in my bed and your appearance has interrupted something special.'

'Jesus, I'm sorry.'

She advances and puts her arms around me and gives me a big hug. 'You're jealous?'

Of course I am but I don't want to admit it. 'You feel good. Do you have somebody here?'

'No, I just wanted to see your reaction. I saw you kissing another woman in Bondi Junction yesterday. So explain.'

'I need a drink,' I say.

'Of course you do. So you can lie with impunity.'

'That was Claire who's just returned from a holiday and she's my girlfriend, it appears. But I don't like her.'

'That doesn't make sense.' Jackie walks to the comfortable white three-seater sofa and sits down.

I follow and sit on the sofa but keep my distance. 'I seem to be a different man from what I was previously. I know it sounds strange but I'm questioning everything now and I feel like disentangling myself from business decisions as well as personal ones. Does that sound daft?'

'It's different, I must say, but as far as I could tell you're going to have a hard time disentangling yourself from the woman I saw you with.'

'Yeah,' I admit. 'It's going to take some effort. I mean, I don't want to be unkind. We obviously had something going for us in the past. It's just that I don't feel anything for her now.'

Jackie comes closer and with her right hand touches my cheek. 'You poor man! Having all these women wanting something from you.'

'You're making fun of me,' I say.

She puts her lips to mine softly and we kiss. When I slide my hands over her thighs she takes them in hers and then peers at me. 'Not so fast. I appreciate the dilemma you're in but I don't want to take advantage of someone who's not entirely together. When you finally regain your memory you may feel differently and want to be with your old girlfriend. And I've been hurt too many times to go through rejection again.'

I sit up straight. 'That's fair,' I say. I cannot continue to make excuses. I'll have to work on getting better, health-wise, although it's frustrating that nobody can help me with a possible time frame. And it's possibly true that I may see matters in a changed light if I ever recover my memory. I stand, kiss Jackie on the cheek, and leave.

At 4:22 am, I wake up in a sweat. The man in black-framed glasses and bushy moustache has again featured in my dream. The man called Leo. The man Claire knows. I get up and splash water on my face. I examine myself in the mirror. I look ghastly, like I've seen a ghost. Perhaps I need to find this Leo. Claire would be able to help through her brother James. I return to bed but resolve that that will be my next job, to find the mysterious Leo and to understand why I appear to be frightened of him. If he was my partner in the creation of new technology, why would he be a threat?

Saturday morning greets me with sunshine and warmth. It's a pity I've chosen not to play cricket because it's a perfect day for it. But I do have more important matters to sort out. I go to my regular café for breakfast, not just coffee. I nod hello to Julie who is busy with another customer. She eventually comes over and we chat about our week. Julie is in a positive mood, having met a new guy the night before.

'That's great news, Julie – for you but not for me,' I say to tease her.

'Go on. When you're serious you let me know, Mr Casanova,' she says, leaving me to the dregs of my coffee.

On my walk home I call Claire.

'Yes,' she says, still smarting from yesterday's conversation.

'Where's James today?' I ask, not really interested in dealing with her tantrum.

'How should I know?'

'Look, I'm sorry about yesterday. Let's not fight. Why don't we get together tonight? But first I need to find James.'

Her manner softens. 'James is at Susan's place. She's his new girlfriend.'

'Where's that?'

'Dover Heights. Give him a call.'

'I've lost his number,' I say, hoping she doesn't ask too many questions.

She gives me his number and Susan's address. I thank her and make a date to meet that night. This is a start in the quest of finding Leo. Dover Heights isn't far from me, I discover, and it will be better to talk with James face to face.

Dover Heights, according to my map, is next to Rose Bay on the ocean side of the Eastern Suburbs and thus a few minutes away by car. I find Susan's flat in Oceanview Avenue easily enough and stand outside the wooden door waiting for a response to my knock.

A woman who I presume is Susan appears as I study the corridor behind her. She is a thin woman with dark frizzy hair and a pointy face. 'Yes?'

'Sorry to intrude but I was wondering whether I could speak with James.'

'Sure, come in,' she says leading me into a spacious area with a fabulous view of the ocean.

James looks up from the paper he's reading. 'Hey dude, how are ya?'

'Not bad. Sorry to barge in like this but I was hoping to have a private chat for a few minutes,' I say, noting that James is slouched and appearing comfortable on the sofa. He is wearing a white tank top.

James stands and leads me out onto the balcony. He is a thin man with sandy hair and a large blue tattoo on his right bicep. 'So what's up? That sister of mine causing you trouble?' He smirks as though he wouldn't be surprised.

'Actually, it's about Leo.' I wait. Does this name mean anything to James? Has he kept in contact with him?

'Leo. I haven't seen him since I've come back from South America. But he's after you, I know. Luckily he doesn't know where you live because Claire asked me to keep it from him.'

'Why's he after me?'

'Something to do with the deal you did with Apple. He's not happy about it. He goes to The Anchor a lot to see if you're around.'

'What did I do to annoy him?' I look out towards the ocean wondering how to tackle this matter.

'No idea. He's so intense. We don't hang out much these days so best of luck with him.'

'Do you know where I can find him?'

James places his hand on the handrail and stares out to sea. Sunlight reflects off the waves, creating a shimmering vista. 'I've lost touch with him but you could try Star City Casino. He loves to gamble.'

***

Star City Casino is an enormous complex in Pyrmont across from Darling Harbour. I find a park and wander around taking in the sights. Multitudes of people are about as it's a late Saturday afternoon. There are restaurants, shops, entertainment venues and of course the main attraction, the casino. I walk through. I may have been here before but I can't remember. There are rows and rows of poker machines and all the seats appear to be taken. I find the tables for Blackjack and roulette. Nobody resembles Leo. Perhaps it's his day off. Perhaps he is too broke to gamble any more. I pass all types of people, well dressed and otherwise. They range from young to very old. Some are watching, some are sitting at tables with serious faces. Some appear jubilant, but most seem sad.

After having surveyed all corners of the casino and eating areas, I feel it's time to go home. I'm not interested in losing money. What a waste of time. I have no inclination to try my luck at anything. I walk back and glance along the rows of poker machines. Here sit the more desperate gamblers, I feel. They appear to be older types who are settling in for the duration. What joy are they seeking? Then, at the penultimate row, I stop. About halfway down is a man who looks like Leo. I move closer and see that it's him. The man of my nightmares. Definitely the one.

Chapter 25 Saturday

The man with the moustache is choking me. He is in front of me with his big hands around my throat. I can see his huge black-rimmed spectacles on his pasty face. I begin to see colours swirling through my mind and it dawns on me that he wants to kill me. He seems stronger than usual and I suspect he's on ice. Suddenly my training kicks in and I knee him in the groin. I grab one of his wrists and twist and shove him away. He falls down. Although he is heavier than I am, I had undertaken a special training course and now that he is on the ground without a weapon he is no match for me.

Something in my mind flashes like a lightning strike. The next moment I'm dazed and I recognise and know who Leo is. That memory of Leo trying to throttle me brings it all back. I step back to observe him. Nobody seems to notice anything, all focussed on the poker machines in front of them.

I've been here before. I recognise the venue. I walk away and find a café. I order coffee and sit down. My memory seems to have returned. I need to check before I get too excited. Yes, my mother is away and she'd told me where she was going and what plans she had for the trip. That's a start. My dad died. Right. That was years ago. My coffee arrives and I take a sugar satchel and empty it into my mug.

I rub my head, which is still somewhat dazed. I now recall the episode with Leo. Leo Jankowski. He has little common sense and poor people skills but he's a genius at programming. Together we created a phone app and he felt his share should have been more than fifty per cent of the amount we negotiated – or rather, the amount that I negotiated –

for the deal. For the idea I had, he did the programming, but I was the interface between the company, a small IT operation now part of Apple, and ourselves. So one day Leo went nuts, having lost most of his share of the funds, which we'd split fifty/fifty, on horse racing, the pokies and blackjack.

He claimed I should have given him more money and that I had cheated him because he did all the hard work. I told him we had a legally prepared written contract and that he should read it. High on some chemical substance, he went for me. Then when I'd pushed him and he lay on the ground staring up at me, he said he would track me down and kill me. Luckily I never trusted him enough to let him know where I live.

So that was the trauma I suffered. He'd come for me at The Anchor that night but because somebody else was attacking me he left. I guess I should thank him for causing the blackout. If it hadn't occurred I may not have met Jackie. But now, with my memory back, I feel revitalised and I need to relish life again. It's nice to put all the pieces together.

I finish my coffee and wonder whether I should confront the misguided Leo now or wait for a better time. After all, I need to fix it so that I'm not always worried he's lurking around a corner with a weapon of some kind. I return to where Leo was sitting and when I see that he isn't there anymore I'm confused. But now that I've recovered my memory, do I need to worry about it? Finding him and seeing him in the flesh has done the trick. I've been in the casino a few times before, I now recall, and it was either with a mate or a girlfriend for a night out. And once only with Leo after he'd collected his share of the app contract and he wanted to celebrate, insisting we go out to drink and have fun. But I'd had no fun watching him place huge bets on blackjack and losing.

I arrive at my car and something tells me I'm not alone. I turn and there behind me is an Asian man with keys out to unlock his vehicle. God, I'm skittish. I get into my car and drive off, wondering whether Leo had seen me.

At home, I call Jackie and tell her what's transpired over the last few hours. She asks if we can meet so she can talk to me to understand what sort of person I really am. I agree but wonder why she's putting me and my past under a microscope. Nobody else would do this. Or would they? My memory may have returned but it still doesn't help me to understand the fairer sex. Live and learn, I guess. No point in overthinking it.

At 8:10 pm I'm sitting across from Jackie in The Anchor. She has a Campari and soda over ice beside her. I have a bottle of Heineken in front of me.

She says, 'So you still remember me, now that you've retrieved your old memories?'

'Very funny. Anyway I'm here and I can get on with life and hopefully you'll be part of that.' I drink some beer and watch her reaction. Her eyes are especially expressive. Big, bright, dark.

'Tell me about your girlfriend and how you feel about her now that you've recovered your memory,' she says, no doubt wanting intimate details.

'This feels like a job interview.'

'I like you, so if I continue to see you and you leave me, I know you could break my heart.'

'Okay,' I say finishing my beer. 'Claire is someone I met at her brother's birthday party. We talked and there was a connection, I guess. Anyway she called me a few times before I agreed to go out with her. And I like her but I'm not mad about her like I am about you.'

'So what are you going to do?'

Typical. I have to prove myself, it seems. 'I don't know exactly but I'm confident it'll all work out.'

She gazes into the distance. I can't guess what she's thinking. I trust it's good but no doubt that's just being foolishly naïve. Her hair is combed back in a smooth wave. It looks great and being a hairdresser, she always keeps it shiny and fresh. 'Do you intend to carry on with Claire or not?'

Finally the penny drops. She wants me to end it before she has anything to do with me. It seems perfectly reasonable when I think about it but it's hard to do. I could say I'm working on it but she wouldn't believe me. 'I need to tell her it's over. Can you give me a few days?'

'Sure. Just let me know when you've done it.'

'Of course,' I say knowing it's easier said than done. Had I not suffered amnesia and been subsequently rescued by Jackie, this conversation would never have taken place. But I have no regrets about that. It's odd, but I'm certain I want Jackie. The reasons are complex and not something I can articulate. Is that what love is? Inexplicable. Mad. Who knows?

Jackie finishes her Campari and I ask whether she'd like another. She declines, gets up, pecks me on the cheek and disappears, leaving me to fathom her. Life would be less complicated if I were able to get away with lying. But I don't want to do that. I want to be honest with Jackie and have a clear conscience.

More people have entered The Anchor, filling the places of patrons who've left. There's nobody I recognise so I have to decide what's next.

I get another Heineken and think about my plight. There's the article, the murder of Murphy, Antonovich, Leo, and my break up with Claire. Enough issues to consider suicide but I'm stronger than that. It's simply a passing thought. Nearly finished, I feel somebody hovering. I turn to see Leo's dark features inspecting me.

Chapter 26 Saturday

'Well, well Leo.' I say, 'Want to join me?'

Leo's a big man with broad shoulders and a gut straining against his green T-Shirt. His face contorts into a scowl. He takes the seat opposite and glares at me. 'Long time,' he says.

'It has been a while. What have you been up to?'

He grunts in reply.

I move slightly, getting more upright in my chair, and wait for him to say something. He still glares as though I'm supposed to understand what he wants from looking at his ugly body. 'Want a beer?' I ask, to be polite.

'You owe me money,' he says.

'How do you figure that?'

'I did the work, you prick. You only had to do the talking.'

I don't know what to say. He looks like he's spaced out. 'Are you on drugs?'

He rises, pulls a gun from the back of his trousers and points it at me. 'Move,' he orders.

I look around and see that nobody is paying attention. Oh, the glories of a big city. Can't somebody film this on their mobile phone and send a copy viral as well as one to the Bondi police station? I get up and turn towards the door, hoping that at some stage one patron realises it's wrong to be escorted out of a bar with a gun at his back.

He forces me outside and tells me to get into my car. I do as I'm told wondering how unstable he really is. I open the car and get in the driver's seat while he rounds the front of the car, gun pointing at me, and slides into the passenger seat. 'Drive,' he commands.

'Where?'

'Your place,' he snaps.

'I don't keep cash at my place,' I say.

'Just do as you're told,' he says, waving the gun about. Then once he's done with his tirade, he keeps the weapon pointed at my midsection as I drive. Without telling him, I drive in the opposite direction from where I live. Full disclosure at this stage is counterproductive. I find myself on New South Head Road and increase my speed as I go through the tunnel towards the city. Soon we're on William Street, which is always busy. Then without any warning I brake hard and jolt Leo forward. I smash my left fist into his face. The gun goes off and the sound almost deafens me as the bullet shatters the windscreen, flying through it and into a car in the outside lane standing parallel to mine.

I karate chop Leo's wrist and the gun drops to the floor. Before I can take further action, Leo undoes his seatbelt, opens the door and scrambles out. This all takes place in seconds and I haven't got the opportunity to grab Leo. I look to see if the bullet has caused harm to anyone. It appears that the bullet hit the top of the Toyota Kluger beside my vehicle. The couple inside the Kluger are terrified and hunched down. As I check that they are alright, the passenger door opens again and Leo grabs the gun. Just as he takes aim at me, he buckles as a vehicle in the outside lane strikes the Audi's passenger door knocking him off balance. Leo falls and the gun goes down with him.

Sirens suddenly sound, filling the atmosphere with alarm, and I am stuck in traffic. Although I realise I shouldn't run off, I'd like the chance to avoid Leo. Is he going to get up and shoot me? I can't get out on the driver's side quickly so I wait. But Leo doesn't re-emerge. Police arrive and point guns at my car and specifically at Leo. Chaos reigns with horns blaring, people rushing about and cars trapped. I want to get away but I have no choice. Now the police will probably shoot if I attempt escape.

'Hands up,' a police officer yells, his pistol drawn.

I look about to see who's speaking. Nothing. Then I watch as a cop from the side of the vehicle slowly comes forward. The back of Leo's head suddenly appears. He is facing the cops who have their guns trained on him. Then shots explode into the side of my car and Leo. His gun drops. He must have pointed the pistol at them. I wonder how much damage there is to my car but I recall that my car is insured with Budget Direct. Thank God for that.

***

I'm sitting at a desk in front of a police officer, who is taking my statement. I now know that Leo has been killed and won't trouble me again. The scene in William Street is over. Traffic has moved on and my car has been towed away. I was given a lift to the city Police Station with a female police officer. She hoped I wasn't too traumatised to provide information about what had transpired. I said I was shocked but prepared to tell my story. Which I did and it's now been officially recorded.

The cop hands me the statement to read and sign. I check it out and notice a few spelling mistakes but otherwise am satisfied that the information is correct. I sign the document and return it. I leave and catch a taxi home. It's been an ordeal I don't want repeated. This is not the way I want to spend my Saturday nights. Then I recall my talk with Jackie. I call Claire and set up a Sunday lunch date.

Chapter 27 Sunday

Overnight it has rained. The ground smells fresh as though it's been washed and thoroughly cleansed. On my walk to my regular coffee place, I take note of the refreshed streets. The aroma of the grass makes me think of cricket, of the days after a shower with the sun beating down, clearing the small puddles left around the pitch. It's a magical time when the day is rejuvenating from humidity and denseness. I walk with keen deliberation, thinking of the day ahead, of Claire and my past.

I recall meeting Claire at the party. She had been standing with her brother James when I walked in, carrying a bottle of red wine. He introduced me to her and I nodded hello. She looked attractive in a grey dress, which outlined her figure in a pleasing manner. I was also introduced to a few more people before Claire came over to me. She said she'd heard a lot about me from her brother.

'All bad, no doubt,' I said.

'That's what made me want to meet you,' she responded.

From there we fell into an easy conversation and she suggested leaving the party. She drove and took me to her place in Bondi. Her flatmate was out so she organised some drinks and before I knew what hit me we were in bed. From then we dated and enjoyed going out to movies and dinner. I'd never analysed our relationship but would have to say it all flowed smoothly. My only criticism of Claire is that she likes to encourage spending. I remember that she wanted me to buy her jewellery and once, an expensive dress, when we were walking through the Westfield complex in the city. I ignored these requests.

Now as I enjoy my coffee, Julie is hovering. 'Come talk to me,'

I say.

'How are you, Nick?' she says.

'Good. What's new on the boyfriend front?'

'Nothing much. The new guy didn't call back so I'm sticking firm and ignoring men – although my ex wants me back.' Julie looks around to see if she's needed.

'Good for you. It won't be long before somebody else, maybe even a decent bloke, will step up.'

'Like yourself?'

'Ha ha. I'm too old for you,' I say.

'Not in my book,' she says, then wanders off.

This comment strikes me as interesting. One minute I'm a Casanova then suddenly I'm right for her. I do hope she finds somebody soon.

***

Lunch is at the Bondi Trattoria. I'm seated and while I'm waiting for Claire, who lives within walking distance, I review the menu. I like Italian food and Claire does too. I try to think how I can make the whole break-up speech sound plausible. There's no real reason to part except that I don't love her. I like her and she's fun but that's it. No doubt if Jackie hadn't come along I'd continue seeing Claire. A few tables down another couple is beginning to make a scene. The woman is getting loud and accusing the guy of cheating. Soon they are both arguing and then she pours her glass of water over his head. He looks stunned while she walks off.

Claire walks in and passes the enraged female. 'What was that about?'

I stand and kiss her on the cheek. 'Who knows? A disagreement, I guess.'

Claire sits at right angles to me and places her hand over mine. 'Hello.' Her smile lights up her face and I'm wondering if I'll have the courage to tell her what I need to.

We order our meals and wine and I ask what she has planned for today.

'After lunch I was hoping that we might go for a nice drive and then go back to your place for some fun.'

'I see. Great plan but I have some work to get through later,' I say. Now that I'm the man with no memory loss I find it irritating that she has made plans for me too. Would I feel the same if Jackie had said this? I don't know but Claire has certainly made me feel annoyed.

Claire makes a face that signifies disapproval. 'Oh. What do you have to do on a Sunday?'

'I have an article that's overdue.'

'And you couldn't even see me last night. What did you do?'

I tell her the story with Leo. I watch her reaction, which changes from disbelief to shock. 'So Leo's dead?'

'Yes, he's gone. He was out of control.'

'So you couldn't afford to give him some money to ease his pain?'

'No, I couldn't. You seem hell-bent on spending my funds,' I say, interested in hearing her response.

She pushes her dark hair back off her forehead. 'Well, what's money for if it isn't to spend?'

'Maybe that's why you don't have much, because you're always spending.' This is cruel but she needs to hear this.

She pouts. 'Why am I keeping it? Saving it for a rainy day?'

'I guess that's not part of your long-term plan, huh?'

'I don't like your tone. I'm leaving. Have a nice Sunday.' She storms out and, given that this is the second woman who has exited this place in this manner today, I wonder whether this restaurant is now used to it. Our order arrives and I wonder what to do. I eat my meal in peace and reflect on what has just transpired. What does this mean? Will Claire ditch me now? I hope so because I'm a coward when it comes to breaking up and I'd prefer her to be the bad guy. Still, I stop thinking about how I'd like the situation to play out as it may ruin my appetite. I pay the

143

waiter after declining dessert.

As I step outside, I look up and see the sky becoming overcast. I walk along Campbell Parade in a daze, both pleased with the outcome at lunch as well as somewhat disappointed that no conclusion had been reached. Rather than worry about my love life, I should be focussing on the assignment I have.

I realise, that to get to grips with the story, I need to find out more about Antonovich. I think back to my first encounter with the now deceased Don Murphy. He had contacted me by phone and arranged a meeting at Wynyard Park. At first I'd thought he was crazy but I'd agreed reluctantly in case it was a scoop. I met him and thought he was a peculiar man who lacked personality and presence. A typical public servant, I'd thought. So he'd handed me a file and said it was important to keep the contents as well as the meeting confidential. But the story needed to be published, he'd stressed. It was a matter of national security. He'd left after a few minutes and I'd sat on the bench for another minute to digest the bizarre encounter.

I drive back to my apartment with a plan in mind. As I walk up the stairs to the front door I meet Ann, who is returning from my unit.

'Hi, Ann,' I say, giving her a peck on the cheek, as I remember her now. Today she is wearing a frilly top and shorts, and I recall dancing with her at one of her parties ages ago. We were friendly neighbours and Matt was cool about the fact that we were cheek to cheek at times. This was before Linda, and then I realise she's never met Claire. 'Were you coming up to see me?' I ask.

'Yes, I wanted to talk with you. Are you available now?'

'Sure, come in.'

We enter my apartment and I organise a coffee for her. I have Moccona instant coffee and I make one for myself too as I hadn't bothered having a coffee after the disrupted lunch. Ann is settled on the sofa with her legs tucked under her taut bottom. I like Ann, I recall as she has always been straightforward. A no-nonsense kind of gal.

'Nick, what do you know about sexual harassment?'

144

I size her up. 'It's not allowed,' I say, sitting down next to her.

'Yeah I know, but I'm in a spot of bother at work. I have a new boss who keeps staring at me and I don't know whether I should say something like bugger off, or simply ignore it.'

'But he hasn't touched you or made unacceptable comments to you yet?'

'No. Should I say something?'

'What does Matt think?'

'He says I'm being precious, that as long as he doesn't do anything I should ignore him.'

I don't really know what to say. If she wore revealing gear to work I can imagine her gaining attention from male colleagues. 'Is he the only one who stares at you?'

'Others aren't so obvious about it and not so persistent. Perry's a creep.'

'If I hear you right, you don't mind the attention, just not from him.'

'Well, I suppose so.' She shifts her position stretching her legs out.

'If you dress the way you are now, I'm be surprised if you didn't get lots of stares.'

She hits me playfully on the arm. 'Oh you. I wear skirts or slacks to work. You can't help it, can you?'

'I agree with Matt. If he escalates the attention – touching or making inappropriate comments, then I'd talk to Human Relations or whatever you call that department. Otherwise, enjoy being so desirable.' I smile, hoping that I'm offering advice that isn't necessarily legal but practical.

'Thanks, Nick. I guess you're right. I may be making too much of something that is really a non-issue.'

She gets up and I walk her to the door. When I open it Antonovich and two men, his bodyguards, I assume, are standing there. One thug was about to knock.

Chapter 28 Sunday

The men push their way in, forcing Ann to retreat. Ginger Beard smacks her on the bottom. 'Sit down, both of you,' he barks.

We sit on the sofa and Ann settles close to me, our legs touching. I put a protective hand on her bare thigh. The two goons stand either side of an armchair in which Antonovich seats himself. He crosses his legs and leans back, studying us. Up close he is quite imposing – tall and powerfully built. I'd seen him only from a distance at Murphy's house and he was then also dressed in a suit. I wonder whether he always wears a suit or only on business. The suit is expensive looking, probably tailored as it fits him perfectly. A strange thought comes to me: does he wear a suit to bed?

'Your wife has nice legs,' says Ginger Beard.

'Keep quiet, Nikolai,' Antonovich snaps. He puts a cigarette in his mouth.

'No smoking in here,' I say.

Antonovich ignores me and lights up. 'Mr Hunter, do me the courtesy of listening if you wish no harm to come to you and your wife.'

'I'm not his wife,' says Ann, who places her hand over mine.

'Don't interrupt. I will do the talking and you will only answer when I ask a question. Is that understood?'

I nod, as I don't want any harm to come to Ann – or myself, for that matter. As I haven't already been killed by his bodyguards, I gather Antonovich wants something from me.

Ginger – or Nikolai, if that's his name – and his silent offsider keep their eyes glued on us. I wait for Antonovich's next utterance. This guy takes himself seriously. I suspect the tough guys are carrying weapons otherwise I'd take my chances in hand-to-hand combat. I recall more stuff now. I did leave the country at times when I was living with Linda. I was trained in combat techniques in Russia, as a consequence of following a story and understanding the individuals who participate in such practices, and hence I held a Russian passport, in a fictitious name. I even learned a few words in that language, which means Antonovich may say things to his comrades without knowing I can understand. Naturally, I'll keep that knowledge to myself.

'Tell me why the article on selling uranium to the Arabs hasn't been printed,' Antonovich says when silence is restored.

What do I admit? That I'm still checking it out? That I don't believe it? That I don't write when pushed around by jerks like him? I say, 'The deadline has been pushed back because of additional research I'm doing.'

'What do you have to research?'

This is my opportunity to seek some truths. 'Who in the Middle East is the recipient of this material? And I don't mean the name of a group like ISIL, but the name of an individual?' Ann squeezes my hand. I sense she is frightened and wants me to play possum.

'Why do you need that?' Antonovich's thick eyebrows twitch.

'To make the story plausible,' I say. I pause to let this sink in and when he doesn't respond I add, 'What's your role in all this?'

'That is not your concern. You need to report to the Australian people that you have corrupt politicians.'

'I think they all know that.'

'I'm not going to argue with you. If I don't see the article in next Sunday's paper I can't guarantee your wife will keep her pretty looks.'

Ann is clearly afraid, judging by the increased pressure she's applying to my hand. 'Give it another week because the newspaper needs to edit it first and I can only deliver the completed piece by Thursday or Friday.'

The three men eye me carefully, probably trying to figure

whether I'm bluffing. 'Make sure it's no later,' Antonovich says.

'Sure, I'll push the editor.'

'Just get it done.'

I don't respond, watching his expression closely.

Antonovich stands, his face impassive, and he and his goons walk out, closing the door gently behind them.

'You're going to write the piece, aren't you?' says Ann.

'Don't worry, I won't let anything happen to you.'

She comes to me, puts her hands each side of my face, leans up and kisses me. 'You're lovely,' she says. She departs, leaving me to ponder options.

I could comply and send off my article, which is largely finished, but I'm still uncomfortable with a number of facts. But should I worry about the facts when lives are under threat? I need to think this through. I call Jackie.

***

Jackie and I are in her bed, spooning, and I have my arms around her, one hand clasped on her left breast, as she is facing towards the door. 'If I were a smoker this would be the time to light up,' I say.

'So you can remember you're not a smoker of cigarettes or weed?' she responds.

'It looks like my memory has completely recovered.' I kiss her shoulder. Having unburdened myself with what had transpired with Claire and Leo, and also the incident with Antonovich, I feel much relieved. Once Jackie had finished listening to my stories and appreciated the danger I'm in, she'd taken my hand and had led me to where I first became aware of my new beginning, her bed. Maybe she'd felt sorry for me because I'd almost been killed, or maybe she'd realised I love her and not Claire, or maybe she'd just been horny. Whatever the reason, it doesn't matter because we are together again.

'What are you going to do about the Russian?'

'What would you do?' I want to get her perspective although I have an inkling about how to proceed.

'I'd go to the police. This man threatened you and this woman.'

'I doubt they could do much. No crime has been committed and it's their word against ours.'

Jackie rolls over and lies on her back. I rearrange my limbs accordingly. 'I find it amusing that there are so many different women in your life and that they think this woman, Ann or whatever, is your wife.'

'I can't help my past but I can control my future,' I say.

'You could hire a bodyguard.'

'Fancy some coffee? I need to thrash out an idea with you and I can't do it with you naked.'

Jackie laughs. 'You can't think in bed?'

'Not next to a beautiful naked woman, I can't.' I get up and dress.

Minutes later we are at the kitchen table enjoying coffee and scones. I explain my idea and we discuss modifications to it. She seems pleased I've confided in her and let her be part of the plan I've formulated. Now we need to put it into operation.

Chapter 29 Monday

After leaving Jackie's, I arrive at my apartment, happy and relaxed. It's 8 am. We'd had breakfast together and then Jackie had gone off to work. Now I shower and get ready for the day. I find myself humming a tune, which is so unlike me. Thinking of Antonovich's insistence that I publish the story Murphy passed on to me, I realise that somebody will be damaged by the information contained in the article. Who is the target? The former defence minister? The Liberal Party? I don't know, but this is the question I need to explore.

After my shower, I call Maxine. I feel exhilarated but I'm not sure if this is the result of my enthusiasm for the project or my memory of the previous night with Jackie. Maxine answers on the third ring. 'Hello,' she says.

'Maxine, I need to meet with you again,' I say.

We fix a time and place for later in the day. As I drive to Pyrmont, I recall my first meeting with Maxine. It had taken place at a media function where a pal of my mine, Paul Drexner, had introduced us. Maxine had shaken my hand and we had chatted about media personalities until Paul excused himself to speak with someone he knew. Once we were alone, Maxine had asked, 'What are you working on?'

'Well, although I'm freelance and work on a variety of assignments, my interest is in investigative journalism,' I'd said, finishing my glass of white wine, which was something akin to vinegar. In fact, I recall wondering why I hadn't taken a beer from the tray carried by the waiters roaming the room. I also remember that I'd mentioned a few articles I had produced for different publications, and that Maxine had seemed favourably impressed.

'Give me a buzz the next time you have something with some substance,' she'd said, handing me a card.

'Thanks,' I'd replied.

Maxine had been wearing a tight black dress that plunged to the waist at the back to reveal well-toned skin and finely sculptured arms. She was older than me, I'd noted, while watching her select another glass of champagne from a passing waiter. As she took mouthfuls of drink she'd begun to flirt with me. When she'd emptied her glass, I'd offered to get us another drink, but she'd said she had a better idea. She'd then grabbed my hand and pulled me outside, where she hailed a taxi. Thirty minutes later she and I were disrobing in her Elizabeth Bay apartment. As we were both a little under the weather, we'd made love on top of her sheets before finally getting under them.

Now I'm facing the curly-haired Maxine across a table in a café in Pyrmont. I order coffees for us and as the waitress leaves, I look at Maxine, who is suitably glamorous in a tight-fitting business suit. I recall how the assignment had come about. I'd called her and pitched the outline of the story and she'd agreed without much further explanation. She said her newspaper had always received good material from me and that she was comfortable with the quality of my writing as long as the subject was something readers found entertaining or scandalous. This story fitted both categories.

'What can I do for you, Nick?' she asks.

'There have been developments that have made the story different from the one I originally presented to you, and I wanted to tell you before you received the material.'

'I see. Will it still expose powerful people?'

'Yes,' I say. 'I also need a favour.'

'What kind of favour?'

'I'd like to work with one of your researchers as I don't have much time to complete the article.'

'I can extend the deadline if the stuff is good,' she says, looking mystified.

I explain without giving away names that lives could be in danger if the article doesn't appear in the weekend or Sunday edition after the upcoming weekend. She doesn't push for additional information, saying that the only criteria for the story to be published will be its quality and newsworthiness.

'Absolutely,' I say. 'I simply wanted to confirm you'll have the space. I'll deliver the completed piece by this Friday, which will give you a week to carry out any editing. Okay?'

'Good. Here's the name of our researcher and this is his direct line,' she says, scribbling the details on a napkin. 'I'll have to get back to the office and I'll tell Stan to expect a call from you. Why don't we catch up in a few weeks once this whole thing is done?'

Although I'm going to remain faithful to Jackie, I agree. We finish our coffee and go our separate ways.

At home I'm about to call Stan to discuss the research I need taken care of when another call comes through. It's Jasmine.

'Remember me?' she says.

'Of course. Been to any other weddings?' The night with Jasmine had been a lot of fun but now I'm not in a mindset to invite her out. Still I'm curious as to why she has called.

'No, I haven't. Not that I've had much time. My flight schedules have been gruelling.'

I sit down, wondering if this is going to be a long conversation. 'So you're back in Sydney for a few days?'

'Two days then I'm off again. I want to see you. I think I have a story that may interest you.'

Intrigued but not convinced, I say, 'Really. What's it about?'

'I'd rather not speak on the phone. Could you pop over tonight?'

I'm torn. I should decline because I don't trust myself with such a beauty, but then again my curiosity has grown in the few moments since she mentioned a story. Surely the meeting can go on without any hitch. 'Okay, I say. What time?'

'Around seven? I'll make you dinner.'

I agree then wonder why I agreed to dinner. Is this my problem? Am I a sex addict? Is there a cure? I dismiss the thought, realising there are far worse problems.

At 7:10 pm, champagne bottle in hand, I knock on Jasmine's flat in a small unit block in Landenburg Place. It had taken me longer to get to Greenwich than I anticipated. After a moment the door opens and Jasmine's bright smile greets me. She walks ahead and I watch as her hips sway. I'm not sure whether this is deliberate or not but I enjoy the vision. She is wearing a long skirt with a slit down the right side, her long legs visible every now and then. Her creamy complexion is flawless, suitable for any clear skin or soap advertisement. She is tall tonight in high-heeled sandals, and I wonder whether she is trying to seduce me before dinner.

When we get to the dining area, I hand her the bottle of Bollinger. The place is tidier than I witnessed on my previous visit, so maybe she's making a special effort. She asks me to open the champagne and I oblige, watching as she obtains two flutes from the glassware cabinet. She invites me onto the balcony and we clink glasses and admire the water views, the harbour bridge in the distance.

'Here's to us,' she says.

'And Monday night,' I add, relishing the moment.

'I love Sydney but I don't get to be here much.'

'What flights are you due on next?' In the evening light I get a fresh view of Jasmine. She is truly beautiful and I wonder why she doesn't have a regular boyfriend.

'Trips to the States mainly. I've just been on the Asia routes and I'm sick of Asian cuisine. So tonight I've prepared some plain steak and potatoes. Hope you don't mind.'

'Not at all,' I say. We finish our champagne and I wander inside and grab the bottle. When I return she is seated, looking out into the distance, and I wonder what she has to tell me. But I wait. No need to hurry anything, particularly as this is such a pleasant experience.

'Nick, I'm lonely. It's probably the job but I can't seem to connect with anyone.'

'Really? I would have thought you'd have no difficulty meeting people and developing relationships, particularly in your kind of job.'

'It's not as glamorous as people think. Sure, I get to see the world and meet people but nothing is long term. Maybe I'm getting old.'

I fill her glass and then mine. I sit in a plastic chair and face her. 'You're probably just having a down day. We all do. In fact, when I met you at the wedding, I didn't know who I was.'

'You're just trying to make me feel good. Let's have dinner.' She stands and leads the way.

I see that telling her the truth about my situation didn't raise any questions. I'm asked to take a seat while she serves. It turns out to be plain but very delicious. The steak is perfect with the mustards and sauces added. The potatoes are crisp, baked just right. A green salad rounds off the meal nicely. She also pours red wine and I note that it is foreign, either Italian or French.

While having a coffee afterwards, Jasmine tells me about what she suspects of a few flight attendants smuggling drugs into Australia. I quiz her and it appears she has no real proof but has a hunch based simply on the apparent wealth of some of her colleagues.

'I can't write a story unless I have concrete facts,' I say.

'I've read lots of newspaper articles that are totally fictitious.'

'In the tabloids perhaps, but I want to maintain my reputation as a journalist of integrity.'

Jasmine comes over and sits on my lap. 'You are so stuffy,' she says cheekily. She puts her arms around my shoulders and pushes her breasts against my face. I want to resist. I want to stay faithful to Jackie but the pressure is unbearable. I slide down into the sofa and surrender, allowing her do what she wants. I am hopeless, I realise, and I need to seek help. But that will come later. For now I let her lead me into the bedroom. She undoes the knot at the top of her dress and it slips off. I am mesmerised by her shape. Soon I am kissing her all over and when I awake the next morning I regret that I've let myself be seduced, but what can I say? I'm a male slut and I love it.

Back at home I realise I must confess to Jackie and not string her along. It's a tough assignment. I call her and she's happy to hear from me. I arrange a luncheon.

Chapter 30 Tuesday

After breakfast I look online for sex addiction sites. Reading them, I find that I don't exhibit tendencies such as exhibitionism, voyeurism or a need to have excessive sexual pursuits. I don't feel a compulsion to masturbate or have sex; I just enjoy physical contact with desirable women. I shut down the sites. I'm not a sex addict, simply a red-blooded male. I wonder if I shouldn't tell Jackie about Jasmine but then I realise it might break her heart if she found out in some other way. I need to be honest with her, irrespective of the consequences. I like her too much not to treat her with respect.

Naturally I want to continue seeing Jackie, but at the same time if she rejects me I'll have to take matters as they come. I realise if I were to have a relationship with any one woman it might end up in marriage or living with that person. And, looking at longer-term relationships among my friends – sure, the first few years appear to be sweet, but I haven't noticed too many successful unions.

I take a bottle of orange juice from the fridge, walk out to the balcony and gaze out at the bay. I can recall three mates who got married young. Ben Jarvis, an old school chum, was married at age twenty-two. After five years he and Jodie went their separate ways. He said the constant nagging broke the spirit of the relationship. Alice Thornton, who I knew at university, got married at twenty-three. She and Tim were happy for a while. Then a child came into their lives. Tim couldn't hack it and began drinking and eventually got abusive. Alice escaped to her parents and she told me she couldn't see herself getting involved with another man.

The breeze brushes my face and the day promises to be bright and cloudless. Finally, I dwell on Bruce Capel, whose partnership with Kate appeared the perfect match. They both came from similar hardworking backgrounds. They had many things in common, the love of camping, sailing and trekking through forests. But something happened after the third child. Then Kate wanted Bruce to disappear and not have any contact with his kids. Bruce loved the children and he couldn't figure why she lied and obtained AVOs and told the police he was violent. Bruce began to doubt himself and took to drugs. Currently he is wandering around somewhere and none of his friends have seen him for eighteen months. A tragic case.

So I don't want to pursue any relationship unless I genuinely understand the other party. Going into a partnership with hidden problems or agendas is a recipe for disaster. I go back to my laptop and re-read what I have managed to put together. But the article will take a different turn from the original one of implicating a former defence minister. I rework it and then wait for my research contact, Stanley Bell, with whom I'd left a message, to call to confirm a number of facts. Just as I finish the revamp my mobile buzzes. It's Jackie and she says an emergency has cropped up and asked that we postpone lunch until tomorrow. I agree, although I'm disappointed.

Then Claire calls. She seems annoyed but insists we get together to talk. I try to dissuade her but after a brief discussion I agree to meet her in the evening.

***

Claire's flat is small. More like two bedrooms and a general area that contains a kitchen, lounge and dining room. Oh, and there's a bathroom squeezed in somewhere. No wonder she doesn't like to entertain here. But we're not here for long. Her flatmate, a woman of forty or so, is at home watching television with a TV dinner on her lap. She doesn't look up when I enter and there is no talk as Claire fusses about to collect her handbag and phone and keys. She also ignores the woman whose name is Mary or Maria or something. We leave with nobody saying a word. I wonder whether they've had a fight or perhaps this is normal. I'd only seen the flatmate once before, and on that occasion she'd been on her way out of the flat as I arrived.

'I've booked a place,' Claire says as she hurries down the stairs, me following. It seems she wants to get out of here desperately. It's only when we've reached the restaurant, which is almost empty, that Claire can sigh with relief. 'I need a drink,' she says.

I order a gin and tonic for Claire and a Heineken for myself. Then I look at her, wondering what's next. She doesn't seem to be in a good mood. We wait until the drinks are served before there is any conversation, Claire meddling with stuff in her bag while I glance around. 'Bad day?' I ask.

'Don't ask,' she says even though I've already asked.

'What's up with Mary?'

'It's Magda. And she and I have had words.'

'Which ones?' I ask, trying to keep things light. I take a mouthful of beer. It tastes good.

Claire glares at me. 'You're not funny. Anyway we need to talk.'

'And have something to eat, I hope. Why is it so quiet in here? Tuesday night?'

'Probably. There's a menu on the table to your right,' she commands. 'Let's order then I need to get something off my chest.'

This doesn't sound good. As I'm inspecting the menu I can only imagine the discussion will give me indigestion. Perhaps I should make an excuse and leave. But that would be cowardly. I order a salad so that my stomach can't get too upset. Claire orders something with chips. I know she likes chips. Her family must have originated in England somewhere. 'Okay, shoot,' I say and hope she doesn't take this literally.

'Ever since I've returned from holiday you've been acting strangely. I don't know what's up but I expect more from you. I'm your girlfriend and I don't like being second place to your work or sport or whatever. You need to tell me everything about what's going on. I know I stormed out the other day and I've thought about it. It was impulsive but you haven't bothered to call and apologise or anything.'

I wait to see if there's more. I could lie but that would only delay the inevitable. Now I see Claire in a different light and it's not flattering. I wonder if I should disclose what has actually happened to me while she was away in South America but I suspect that it would be beside the point. She's not really interested in me but simply in how it impacts on her. 'I've had a lot on my mind,' I say, which I know is feeble but I'd like to get through dinner first. Surely this sort of confrontational discussion is best left for later, during or after coffee. But she's obviously of a different mind.

'That doesn't cut it, I'm afraid. Unless you share with me I think you may need to reconsider this relationship.'

Fantastic, I think. She may break up with me so that I won't have to do the dirty work. I finish my drink and then get the waiter to bring another round. If Claire has more alcohol she may calm down a bit. The expression on her face looks like a volcano ready to erupt. 'You know I've been working on a sensitive assignment.'

'I did not know,' she stammers. 'That's what I'm talking about. You've been secretive and I can't live with that.'

The drinks arrive and I realise I need this more than I thought. 'Let me fill you in.'

'I don't want the details now. Why does your work interfere with the fun we should be having? You know, like going to parties and nightclubs like we used to?'

I recall going to the occasional nightclub and some parties but she is exaggerating. She is imagining we had an idyllic existence and forgetting that the early months of any relationship are usually just fun. The same happened when I was with Linda. Great for three or four months then bang, disappointment. Well maybe not that dramatic but certainly changes do occur and that's the time to assess how things are progressing. 'I don't know,' I say, which I know is poor, but I'm waiting for her to make the move to end it.

'Is something else going on?'

This interrogation is torture. I have to come clean. 'I've met somebody else.'

'You what? In the few weeks I've been away you've gone out and picked up another woman?' She looks ready to explode.

'It wasn't like that. I was in trouble and she helped me.'

'Okay, she helped you out, so why does that mean you're now going out with her?'

'I love her,' I say. This is a revelation my mind has denied but somehow it flew out of my mouth.

Claire gets to her feet, picks up her glass of water and tosses it in my face. She departs, leaving me with a wet face and shirt. I pay the bill and go outside without eating. Well, that went well, I say to myself. Now it'll be Jackie's turn for anger and indignation tomorrow.

Chapter 31 Wednesday

I wake on Wednesday morning feeling awful. Although I had to do what I had to do, the outcome wasn't what I wanted. I guess breakups are never going to go smoothly. I have breakfast, pondering life. It seems I didn't know Claire that well. Sure, the news I presented wasn't what she wanted to hear, but the reaction was something I didn't foresee. I don't think I'd react like that if a woman I was keen on broke up with me. But perhaps I'm wrong. Women have broken up with me in the past and I handled it. But did I really love any woman like I do Jackie? That will be the test. And I'll find out soon enough.

Lunch is at the Osteria Riva Restaurant in Bronte Road, Bondi Junction. Jackie's recommendation. It is an overcast day, clouds threatening to pour forth with tons of wetness. I didn't bother with an umbrella so if it rains I have quite a walk to get to my car. But that's the least of my worries.

I arrive seconds after Jackie, who is strolling down to a table. She looks magnificent in a black frilly top, a leather miniskirt and black high heels. She is more woman than the svelte curvy Jasmine but utterly fabulous nevertheless. Before she sits down I catch up to her and give her a hug. She responds by hugging me back and kissing me on the cheek. We sit down across from each other. I look into her eyes, which are so beautiful and seem larger than those of any other woman I've known. I need to choose my words carefully. I still waver over telling her about Jasmine.

We chat about her hairdressing business, which seems to be back on track. Then we talk about my work and the deadline I've imposed. During this time we order coffee and food. Finally our meals arrive and everything goes well – no drama, no conflict. We eat and I'm conscious that it's best to keep the key issues for discussion until after our meal. After all I don't want to have coffee poured over me. Not only will it be hot but it will ruin my clean top, a new Nautica black shirt.

'I've broken up with Claire,' I say.

'I see,' Jackie says, watching me carefully. 'It's your business but was it what you wanted or do you feel I pressured you?'

This is an interesting question. I pour myself a glass of water and offer Jackie some but she has enough in her glass and declines. Outside it is raining and I wonder whether I can answer so that I don't have to go out to experience the weather just yet. A couple shaking umbrellas wanders past our table. Finally I say, 'I realised the relationship wasn't built on anything except mutual fun times. I didn't love Claire and it was unfair to string her along.'

Jackie is silent but the look on her face signifies approval, at least in the sense that what I've said makes sense. I breathe a little easier. My shirt is still dry. Then I continue, 'I also have a confession. I've messed up recently and it won't happen again, but I'd like us to continue to see each other in an atmosphere of trust.'

'What's that mean?'

'I slept with someone else. As I said – a mistake.'

Now Jackie's expression resembles the darkness outside, thunderous clouds building in her face. So far no waterworks. Either she doesn't care or she doesn't tear easily. I'm holding my breath.

'You can't help yourself, can you?'

'Let me explain,' I respond.

She stands. 'I'm disappointed but I shouldn't be. You're all the same. You think with the lower part of your brain.' She storms off and at the exit, draws a small umbrella from her bag. She opens the apparatus as she steps out into the now strong rain.

So here I am alone. I've not handled it well. Losing a girlfriend and lover in twenty-four hours is something I haven't managed before.

It's probably a record of some sorts. All I have to look forward to now are thugs and work pressure. Perhaps it's best that my romantic entanglements are over. I may be able to concentrate on business better.

**

Stanley Bell calls just as I reach home and close the door, my body drenched from the rain. He says Maxine wants him to work with me and that he is at my disposal. I outline some areas I need to check out. He says he'll get in touch as soon as he has the necessary information. I don't know Stan but he appears professional. I have a shower and change my clothes. Now that I have no female distractions I can focus on my work.

I reread my article and edit certain sections. The research should confirm certain facts but it's still too early to judge. Having done that, I look at the time and see it's nearly six o'clock. I think about dinner. I'm hungry now, as I hadn't bothered with lunch. I could make something or go out by myself. But neither option appeals.

A knock on the door interrupts my ponderings. I walk to the door wondering who it could be, seeing as I've pissed off most of the people close to me. I look through the peephole. Nobody there. I hope it's not Antonovich and his dumb mates. I open the door and my mother suddenly appears from the side. She seems to have picked up a piece of paper, which was floating about.

'Hello mum,' I say, giving her a hug. 'Come in.'

She follows me in and I close the door. 'How are you, son?'

'Great. What are you doing back? I wasn't expecting you until next week.'

My mother is a slight woman but has looked after herself and doesn't look her age, which is fifty-seven. 'I know. I came back early. I want to talk to you about something. Why don't we go out to eat? I know you don't like cooking.'

'Sounds good. Let me take you to one of your favourites in

Watsons Bay.'

'You're a good son,' she says, handing me a gift.

'Thanks Mum, you shouldn't have. What is it?'

'Open it,' she says.

I do as she suggests. It turns out to be a box of chopsticks.

***

We're seated in The Tea Garden, Watsons Bay, which overlooks the water. My mother has a cup of tea in front of her while I have a glass of red wine sitting to my right. We have ordered a meal and my mother has filled me in on her vacation. Finally she gets to the point of the outing.

'I've met someone,' she says.

'Good,' I say. 'I'd expect you would on your exotic travels.'

'Yes silly, but I'm talking about a man who I'm going to keep seeing. He's also from Sydney.'

'Really. Where did you meet?'

'On a tour bus. We were sitting next to each other. After a while we got chatting and we just continued talking throughout the tour and then that evening. He was such fun and we just seemed to click.'

I don't really know whether she wants me to say anything or whether she simply wants to tell me the news. I think it's best to be encouraging. Since my dad died mum has been morose. Apart from her recent adventure, she hasn't done much at all to amuse herself. 'That's great. Is this guy retired?'

'Sort of. Apparently he still consults on and off.'

'Oh yeah. So he's well off?' I need to know he's not after her money. My dad left her with a considerable estate.

'Oh yes. He lives by himself in Mosman. He's a widower.'

'Perfect,' I say, knowing that he must be loaded if he lives in Mosman. I don't want to pry too much but I hope he has a nice house overlooking Balmoral Beach. 'And he's around your age?'

Mum asks for more tea when a waiter approaches with our meals. When the surly young man departs, she says, 'He's fifty-eight. Still looks fit and plays golf.'

We eat. Mum has a salad and eats slowly. I have an appetite now and demolish my pasta. When I finish I look outside at the fabulous view. Now that the rain has stopped the remnants of sunshine provide a shimmering vision of water and city vistas.

'How's Claire?' she asks out of the blue.

'We've broken up.'

She looks up at me. 'I'm not disappointed, Nick. I didn't think she was right for you.'

This intrigues me as she'd only met Claire once. But I'm not about to get into a discussion about it. Mum has always been critical of my women. 'I'm single and fancy free at the moment.'

'Won't be for long, if I know you. You should think about settling down with a nice woman. You're getting on, you know.'

'I realise I'm getting older but nice women are hard to find,' I say. The last thing I need is advice on romance from my mother. Now that I've broken up with Jackie, I can't bring her up in conversation.

I drive mum home afterwards. Her Bellevue Hill house is the same place I grew up in. She loves it here and I wonder what she will do with her new man. Unlike me she is a stayer, never having known any guy before my father. She asks if I'd like to come in for a cup of tea but I decline.

On my ride home I wonder what will become of me. I seem to have little time for taking life seriously. Perhaps I need a good woman. Thoughts of Jackie emerge but then I remember Antonovich and his threats and think that at least with Jackie out of the picture she can't come to any harm.

Chapter 32 Thursday

Stanley Bell interrupts my daydreaming at my regular coffee place. After waking at my usual time of seven o'clock, I'd had a light breakfast of cereal and had then wandered down to the café where Julie was pleased to see me. For a moment I'd been tempted to invite her out, but soon I discarded the idea. How long would that last? She is so young and I'm beginning to feel old.

'I've got some interesting information for you. Probably best to meet. How are you placed?' Stanley asks.

'I can meet you today, say in an hour or so.'

'Great. You know where I work. There's a café up the road and I'll see you there at 10 o'clock.'

I agree and finish my cappuccino. At this rate I'll be having enough coffee to stay alert for days.

When I arrive at the entrance to the café a man is waiting out-side. He nods hello. Stan is a man much younger than I would have thought from his telephone voice. I guess he'd be around twenty-five. He is thin and wiry, and stands just over six foot. He has a firm handshake. After ordering coffees at the counter, we go to the back of the cafe and sit down.

'That was quick work,' I say.

'It became very interesting when I began to look into it, so I just kept going. Besides, I have a few useful political sources so I had help.'

'Excellent,' I say, noting that Stanley has donned his reading spectacles, and now looks more mature.

'There's a by-election being held in the MP's seat in a month.

And guess who is contesting it?' Stan pauses, awaiting input, but when I don't respond he continues. 'None other than a Magnus Kuklev, your man's brother-in-law.'

'Wow,' I say. So that is Antonovich's motivation. He wants me to smear the current sitting member with a scandal so that his brother-in-law can win the seat. By the time any investigation into the truth is conducted the by-election will be well and truly over.

Stan provides some documents and I thank him. This will be the final nail in Antonovich's coffin. I had already written enough to link him to Don Murphy's murder and he will be most disconcerted when I tie it all in with this information. Obviously, in the article, I don't accuse him of Murphy's murder but I simply make the case that he is the only one with any real motive. Stan and I chat some more then I tell him that Maxine can expect the complete story by tonight. When we part I shake his hand and thank him again for the documents.

At home I prepare to finalise the article. I take a glass of cold water and set it beside my laptop. On the way home I'd planned how I was going to structure the piece. And with no women to interrupt me I should have the entire afternoon to write without distraction. I begin my work and half an hour later my iPhone buzzes. I'm not going to answer it. I check the caller. It's Jackie. What could she want? To abuse me further? I pick up. 'Yes?' I say, wondering whether she's going to berate me some more or whether she's changed her mind and wants to make love to me.

'Nick, I'd like to apologise for yesterday. I guess I got emotional when I had no right to. You were honest and, at the time you did what you did, you had no way of knowing that I'd get back with you,' she says.

I'm not sure how to take this news. 'That's very adult of you,' I say, wondering what this means. Is she going to forgive me or is she simply wanting to part on favourable terms? I look into the distance, pleased on one level but confused as well. Why do women make life so awkward? Perhaps that's what they were designed to do.

'So are you actually involved with anyone?'

'No, not a soul,' I say. I trust that the evening with Jasmine won't inspire her to think we are in a relationship. But what would I know about a female's thinking processes?

'I know that I may seem scatty but I like you and I don't want to throw away the opportunity of building something ...'

I interrupt. 'I agree. Let's talk tonight. I have to finish something by then. What do you say?'

'Fine, I'm game.'

'Great. I'll pick you up at seven.'

With the promise of a brighter future I set about my work with added vigour. At five o'clock I put the final touches on the article, then I send it via email to Maxine. I close my laptop and enjoy a long shower, singing the chorus to a song I'd heard earlier. As I dress I wonder what the implications will be when Antonovich reads the piece, maybe over breakfast. Will he choke? I don't know but Ann and I shouldn't be in danger once the story is told and he is exposed. It's only prior to publishing that there could be an issue.

As I drive towards Bellevue Hill and Jackie's rented flat, I think of more pleasant matters. There is a little drizzle in the air, and it cools down what has been a very warm day. I arrive at Jackie's door at five after seven. I knock and smooth my hair as I wait. No answer. I knock again. When I get the same response I pull out my iPhone and call her number. She might be held up at work or in traffic. But the call isn't answered.

I look out at the street to see the drizzle becoming heavier and in the distance the sky is dark. Now I'm concerned. Jackie is so reliable. Besides, we were in touch only hours before. She'd call if she had to postpone the date. I drive to The Anchor to see whether she'd popped in and somehow forgot what time we'd agreed on. I walk in, leaving the car parked illegally, to see whether Jackie or any of her friends are here. There's no sign of anyone I recognise. I ask the barman whether he's seen Jackie. He shakes his head. Now I'm really worried.

I walk out again, in a daze, not noticing the rain or anything else. I get into the car and find my way home. What can I do? If I call the police they won't take seriously the idea that a nearly thirty-year-old woman is missing after not fronting for a date. I'd be laughed off the premises. They'd imagine she didn't want to see me. They might even consider arresting me for harassing her. I find it difficult to stay calm. I call her number again. When it fails to get an answer I get a bottle of scotch, my last unopened one, and pour some into a glass. I swallow without water, ice or ginger ale. It slides down my throat burning its way right to my stomach. It feels satisfying. I have more.

A noisy buzz awakens me. I sit up, realising I'm slumped on the sofa after falling asleep. I answer the nuisance call.

'Yes?'

'If you'd like to see your woman friend again you better listen and listen good,' a male voice says.

'Who is this?'

Chapter 33 Thursday/Friday

There is a pause at the end of the phone and I wonder if this is a prank call. The male voice continues, 'You were told what to publish. Do it and delete the stuff you sent in. Otherwise Ms Jackie will suffer.'

'Who are you? And where is Jackie?' I am fully awake now and agitated.

'Never you mind. Do what you promised to write.'

I'm furious. I don't know what to do. I know I should contact the police, but having watched a few kidnap movies, I wonder if they'll be of any use. 'I need to know she's okay. Let me talk to her.'

'That's not going to happen.'

'Then you can go fly a kite, I'm not changing a thing unless I get to talk to her.'

The voice pauses a moment. 'I'll call you back.'

I start to think now that I'm off the phone. I stand to let the blood flow. How did anyone know about my article? And the voice sounded strangely artificial, as though somebody was talking through a conduit, muffled by cloth or an instrument to alter the voice. So if it was Antonovich, why did he bother to disguise his voice? Perhaps it's all a game to him. His goons must have been following me, and they must have known about Jackie's location. I've been so stupid going about my business as though nothing was out of the ordinary – and now some thug is set to harm somebody dear to me.

I drink some water and think some more. I sit on the sofa again, feeling restless and helpless. Antonovich has Jackie but then if I call the cops he'll deny it and there will be no proof. That's why he had to cover up any suggestion he might be involved. I can't claim I definitely heard him on the phone. Besides, one of his lackeys may have called. So I'm stuck. I walk out onto the balcony waiting for my phone to ring.

At 9:13 pm I get the call. I note the number isn't disclosed. The voice says, 'Here she is. You have a minute only.'

Jackie comes on the phone, 'Hello, Nick.'

'Darling, are you all right? Have you been hurt?'

'I'm fine, but ... '

The phone is snatched and the voice returns. 'Right. Now destroy what you've written and get the right article in place. You have twenty-four hours.' He hangs up.

I go back inside and sit down. What am I going to do? I would rather have a fake article published than have any harm come to Jackie. But even if I do Antonovich's bidding, how do I know he'll keep his word? I pace up and down, frustrated, angry.

Then I make a rash decision. I get into my car and drive to North Sydney. Traffic is lighter than during the day but still heavy enough to keep the speeding to a minimum. I get to Antonovich's house and park a few places up from it. I walk back to see if there's an obvious place that someone could be held. Lights are on so I have to sneak into the yard hoping there is no dog to alert the inhabitants.

I make my way to the front window without incident. I take the chance of looking inside. I can't see anybody. What I can see is a lounge with a drinks cabinet, two long cream settees, a couple of leather armchairs and a flat screen television on the wall. The television shows pictures of people in a kitchen cooking things. A cooking show, all the rage these days. Like cooking was a novelty that older generations had not discovered. So I realise that someone will come in shortly. Does Antonovich watch cooking? I doubt it. But one never knows.

After waiting a few minutes, occasionally looking around to check nobody is sneaking up on me, I see a young girl of around ten wander into the room. She is followed by an attractive woman of about thirty-five, who brings in a bowl of popcorn. They sit down and watch

171

the cooking exploits on the show. So it's good to know Antonovich has family, people he'd not like to see harmed. As he probably doesn't know I know where he lives, I have a card up my sleeve. I leave the window, watching to ensure nobody is about on the quiet street. With the area clear, I move quietly to my car and drive home.

***

The next morning I wake at my customary time of seven o'clock without any alarm being set. I stretch, pump fifty push-ups, and have a shower. I'm in a jubilant mood for someone whose girlfriend has been taken hostage by a gangster, but I have a plan. My training in Russia will finally pay off. I eat a hearty breakfast and during my walk to the local café I call Maxine.

'Hi Nick, loved the article. There's hardly any editing to do. Are you calling to confirm the release date?'

'No Maxine, I'm in trouble. The article has been leaked to a character named in the piece and I need to know who that might be. Any ideas?'

'Not really. It came to my email address and the only other person who knew about the article is Stan, and I would doubt that he would disclose anything to Mr Antonovich,' she says, sounding bewildered.

'I believe you. Does anyone else get involved in the editing or checking of facts?'

Maxine pauses a moment. 'Leave it with me. I'll talk to Stan.'

The sky is bright blue today and I continue on my way. Julie is in a good mood this morning and we share a few pleasantries. After my coffee I hail a taxi on New South Head Road and ride to my bank, collect my pistol from the safety deposit box and catch another cab home. I check that the gun is working properly. I think about a number of strategies. Although I don't know Antonovich's mobile or home numbers, I call on a police source to carry out a search to obtain his home number. There's no reason to use it but it's always useful to be prepared.

As I ponder the options, Maxine calls. 'Yes?' I say.

'I spoke with Stan and he thinks his email was open when he went outside for a moment to smoke. There could be two or three people who may have seen it. But we don't know who it might have been. Any suggestions?'

'Let me pop over and I'll figure it out,' I say, not convinced it's that easy.

'Okay. Give me a call when you're in the lobby and I'll come downstairs to take you up. It's for security reasons.'

***

The cab drops me in front of the huge L-shaped building. I climb out and get a receipt, as this will end up a business expense. I walk to the entrance and pull out my phone. Maxine, dressed in a black pinstriped skirt and a white shirt, greets me and takes me upstairs in the elevator. We don't talk until we get into her office.

'What's your plan?' she asks.

'I'm hoping Stan can introduce me to the people who may have stolen the article.' I brush fluff off my pale blue business shirt.

'How would they have done that?'

'Probably a USB stick,' I say, not certain but having imagined, during the drive from my place, how it might have happened.

Maxine leads me out and when I'm in Stan's cubicle she asks him, in a voice that can be overheard, to show me around the rest of the office to meet others in the department. She whispers to Stan that I particularly want to meet the three individuals who may have seen the article on his computer.

Maxine leaves us and I ask Stan whether anyone would have noticed someone popping in to his cubicle yesterday. He tells me that the person across the corridor may have seen something. He takes me across and introduces me to Ray Brown. Ray is in the open-plan area and he stands when Stan introduces me. He is a tall skinny man with dark brown hair and a two-day stubble.

'Hello, Ray,' I say. 'Nice to meet you.'

Stan says, 'You didn't see anyone pop into my cubicle yesterday when I went outside for a break, did you?'

'No. Didn't see anything. I may have been away from my desk.'

We move on. Next I'm introduced to Hanna Nilsson who is a plump blonde woman of around forty. 'Hi,' I say.

'Pleased to meet you,' she says and smiles. 'Are you in the research team?'

'He's part of my external research group,' Stan says. 'He won't be in the office much.'

I look around to see if Hanna could have noticed any people wandering into Stan's cubicle. Stan notes my interest and asks her the same question he posed to Ray.

'I think Jay poked his nose in and Kevin did and he seemed to be there a bit longer. Why? Has someone stolen your stapler again?'

'That's right. Trying to track the culprit,' Stan says, playing along.

'Good luck with that,' she says, and then she turns back to her computer screen.

Stan leads me to a meeting room. 'How do you want to proceed?'

I sit down and place my chin on two fingers, looking at Stan who is standing by the door. 'Let's arrange a coffee for the two potential culprits and then we can have a chat with them to suss them out.'

'One at a time?'

'Yes. Good idea. What are their functions?' I sit back, surveying the room.

'Jay is an office boy. He's only been with us for a few months.'

'So he could be a plant, do you think?' I suggest.

'Maybe. But he's not that bright so I have my doubts.' Stan takes the internal phone and speaks to someone to send up some coffee.

'And Kevin?'

174

'Kevin has been around for some time. He's in charge of Features.' Stan hesitates then adds, 'I don't know what motive Kevin would have to leak anything.'

When Kevin comes in I stand, shake his hand, and Stan informs him that I've joined his team as an external research consultant. Kevin is grey haired, ruddy faced and has small beady eyes. I look into them but don't see anything evasive. We all sit down then the coffee jug arrives. A young woman who looks no more than eighteen brings in a tray that contains a coffee pot, cups, a jug of milk, sugar cubes and biscuits. She sets up the cups and places the other items in the middle of the table. I gather she's practised at this. She does her job without looking at us.

Once we've all settled in, I say to Kevin, 'Stan has been kind enough to send me the stuff on that Russian guy and I'm wondering how you'd feel if the article is delayed another few days before you see it.'

'No skin off my nose,' he says.

I sip some coffee. 'Okay. It should be with you either Friday night or over the weekend.'

'What changes are you making?' Kevin keeps his expression neutral but I now know he's seen the original.

'I'm not sure exactly. It's just that some details need to be adjusted.' I watch his reaction, wondering if he knows I think he's the leak. Of course I still need to confirm this, but I have a plan for that, too.

We talk a little more about my supposed role at the newspaper then we let Kevin go. We ask Jay to join us to ensure all the bases are covered. Jay is young, around twenty-two, medium height with close-cut dark hair. He sits opposite me and like Kevin before him, keeps his expression neutral. He waits while I explain my role. But Jay doesn't react to what I say and I wonder if he's clueless or simply a good actor. It's hard to consider him a suspect but you never know. He leaves without saying a word and without bothering with coffee. I thank Stan and tell him I'll be in touch.

I return home. Now the real work begins.

Chapter 34 Friday

I check I have everything – wallet, key ring, sunglasses and gun. I've sent a fake amended article to Maxine, who will pass it on to Stan, who will ensure that anyone seeking to copy it or simply check it out will be caught. A hidden motion activated camera has been set up. Maxine has also agreed to hold a meeting to inform staff that a new version of the article will be forwarded to Stan, who is expected to carry out final integrity checks.

I arrive at Antonovich's house a little before three o'clock. I wait in the car. Antonovich's wife and daughter should be back from school soon, I imagine. Perhaps I should stake out the place a few times to determine what routines the family usually follows but I have insufficient time. I need to find Jackie as soon as possible.

As I sit and watch the few people wander about, I wonder about my strategy. If I kidnap Antonovich's family, am I not as bad as he is? But I have no option, do I? The police won't be able to do anything unless they are called. And Antonovich would deny any wrong doing if I'm captured and am thereby able to explain my reasoning about a kidnapping to them. No, I reason, taking two captives in exchange for Jackie is the only practical solution.

At three-thirty a Mercedes rolls up the street and turns into the Antonovich residence. The vehicle carries two people, a female driver and a young female passenger. I brace myself. I will knock on the door and pretend to be a donation collector. By the time Mrs Antonovich asks questions it will be too late. I wait another couple of minutes and walk to the door. I plan to transfer the couple to their own car and take them to my mother's place as she and her new beau are away for a few days. Once there I will lock them in a room and negotiate a trade.

I know this idea is flawed because Antonovich and his men could easily come after me once his wife and daughter are back with him, but I just need to keep Jackie and myself safe until Sunday, two days away. Maxine has agreed to publish the article this Sunday, not next week as originally scheduled. Once that has happened, Antonovich will have plenty of explaining to do, particularly about the apparent suicide of Donald Murphy.

I arrive at the door and take a deep breath. The actual act of doing what I'm about to do doesn't faze me. The training in Russia has readied me for action. What does concern me is implicating two innocents. If only there was an alternative in the brief time available.

As I'm about to knock a piece of metal is shoved in my ribs.

'Freeze,' says a voice.

I realise it's one of Antonovich's muscle men and the metal digging into my ribs is the barrel of a pistol. I wait for further instructions. I glance sideways and realise it's my old mate 'Ginger Beard'.

'Eyes front,' he says.

'Sorry,' I say. 'It's difficult to carry on a conversation like this.' I know he can't kill me yet because he needs the article to be published, and he also needs permission from his boss.

He knocks on the door and after a short wait a tall brunette opens up. 'What's going on?' she says.

Ginger Beard pushes me inside and I sweep past Mrs Antonovich. Ginger Beard enters and shuts the door. A child comes into the room and says, 'What's happening, Mummy?'

'Yes Nikolai, what's going on?'

Ginger pushes me into a seat. 'He,' he says, 'is a journalist.' He stops, not knowing how to proceed.

'And?' says Mrs Antonovich.

I decide to speak. 'Mrs Antonovich … '

'Katherine,' she says.

'Katherine, my name is Nick Hunter and it's true, I am a journalist. Your husband has engaged me to write an article.'

'So why is Nikolai pointing a gun at you?'

'That's a good question,' I say. 'We've had a few run-ins and he's always come off second best. I guess holding a gun makes him feel more like a man.'

Nikolai snaps, 'Shut up, you piece of dirt.'

I wait for more but it doesn't come. He's obviously a man of few words. A man of action.

'So what are you doing here? My husband is at work.'

'I've come to kidnap you and your daughter,' I say.

Everyone laughs.

While Nikolai is enjoying the joke his gun is temporarily pointing away from me. I take the opportunity to slide off the sofa and using my legs, twist him backwards. He falls and the pistol drops. I pick up the gun and grab Nikolai by the collar so he is standing upright again. I jam the pistol into his ribs. Then I say to Nikolai, 'Now move, out the back.' To the wife I say, We're taking your car, Katherine. Next time you see your husband, ask him about the kidnapping of my girlfriend.'

'What … ' says Katherine, looking shocked and stunned.

I don't respond as I hustle Nikolai forward. The circumstances have given rise to a new plan, which doesn't involve taking the two females. A trio of individuals would be difficult to subdue.

Before further words are exchanged, I push Nikolai forwards, snatching the car keys on the way towards the back door. I force him to drive the Mercedes out of the Antonovich place. The gates luckily haven't yet been closed. I keep the gun low to avoid snoops seeing anything but have it pointed at his midsection.

'Where we go?' he asks.

'Drive up the Pacific Highway. I'll let you know when to turn off,' I say. I need to find out where Jackie is held and I'm sure Nikolai knows. He was probably involved with the kidnapping. As we pass the Union Hotel to our right, I wonder how best to extract the information. I direct him to a park in Greenwich, where I've played cricket. It's called Gore Creek Reserve and it's deserted at this time of day. When we reach the park, I tell him to stop the vehicle near the overhead footbridge. I face him, taking the keys out of the ignition.

He looks at me, a slight smirk on his face.

But he doesn't speak. Maybe he's too macho to show vulnerability. I'd thought of a variety of ways to torture him to gain the information I need. I doubt that beating him would elicit much as he's probably a thug used to physical beatings. He's no doubt had many physical fights and a bunch of bruises over the years. I could tape his hands to the steering wheel and cut off one finger at a time until he confesses Jackie's whereabouts, like in the movie *Man on Fire*, which I've watched at least three times. Instead, I point the pistol at him and tell him to close his eyes. After a moment he complies as he sees from my determined expression I mean business. Then, turning away for the briefest time, I open the pistol and remove bullets, close the pistol, spin the cylinder and point it at Nikolai's head. 'Tell me where you're keeping Jackie,' I say, my eyes focussed on his as he opens them again.

'You're not killer, you're journalist, pen pusher. I don't think you have guts to do dis,' he says, smiling.

I squeeze the trigger. Nothing happens.

'Shall we try again?' I ask, watching him closely for signs of fear. And I note that the expression on his face has changed. The smirk has gone. I wonder what it's like to kill a person. I've had no experience of this and question whether people actually enjoy the prospect of seeing life drain from a living creature. Humans are creatures just like other mammals but some individuals distinguish between the two, dismissing the killing of animals as nothing unusual. I haven't killed an animal and I don't think I want to do such a thing. For me, there's little difference between killing a person and killing another living creature. Life is precious, for all.

'You are mad. Just for a story you do dis?'

'I'm not doing this for a story. I'm wanting to free a kidnapped woman. You realise kidnapping is a federal offence?'

'She will be let go when the story is done.'

'Which brings me to another topic. Who's your contact at the newspaper?'

Nikolai suddenly looks frightened. 'I don't know.'

I squeeze the trigger again. Nothing happens. Now Nikolai looks seriously afraid.

'Oritz … Jay Oritz,' he stammers.

'Now, that wasn't too hard. So tell me where Jackie is being held.'

'She is fine. Bin looked after … you have nothing to worry about,' he splutters.

I wait. He's being stubborn, I know, but slowly his defences are fading. 'Now let's get back to where she is,' I say firmly. I stare at him so he knows I'm not going to give up.

'Antonovich will kill me if I talk.' He's looking sad faced as though this might sway me.

I squeeze the trigger again. 'Not before I kill you,' I say in a ba-dass voice.

'I take you. It's not far.'

I return the keys to him. He starts the vehicle and we drive off. I explain to him on the way that I will kill him should he try anything, anything untoward at all. Ten minutes later we're in Lane Cover in front of a house nestled in a yard overflowing with gardens and trees. It seems isolated with no houses nearby. It's a perfect spot to hide someone.

He stops the car and undoes his seat belt. I gather the discarded bullets from my pants pockets and before I know it Nikolai opens the door and scrambles out. I see him running like a madman, actually more like a scared rabbit, into the bushes. What he didn't know was that I had removed all the bullets and that there was no danger of him being killed. Fear is often more potent than action.

After removing the car keys, I climb out of the passenger-side door and sneak towards the house. I venture down the side and around to the back to examine the layout. The back is close to the bushes but there is a fence. This keeps wildlife away, I suspect. I wonder whether Antonovich is here. What about other bodyguards? I creep along the wall and when a window appears I wait then peek inside. I see nothing. I move along until the back door presents itself. There are steps leading up to it, as the front of the house is higher than the back, with land sloping down from the footpath to the bush beyond. The lawn is mown, suggesting that the place is cared for.

I skip around the steps and move to the next window and again take the chance to peer inside. This time I see someone. It's Nikolai's mate, the other bloke who'd accompanied Antonovich to my flat. So this appears to be the right place. I need to do something before this guy gets tipped off. Would Antonovich's wife warn him? Is she in on it with her husband? I don't know but I need to act fast. I consider my options. Break in and use the gun for leverage? Noisy and dangerous. I dismiss the idea. I could knock on the front door and wait for him to answer? But that could be dumb too, as he would suspect something and come out armed.

While I'm thinking, I wander back to the rear doorsteps and gently ascend them. Perhaps the lock is not too hard to break. Before I take out a credit card to attempt this strategy, I try the handle and to my surprise the door opens inwards. Gun ready, I move inside, as silently as a mouse surveying cheese left on the floor. I'm in a corridor adjacent to the room, which the guard occupies. I creep down the carpeted aisle. As I approach the door to my left, scenes from films invade my thoughts. But this is not a movie and I'm not going to be able to rush into the room, fire and somersault and avoid damage. So I walk slowly and when I reach the opening I simply emerge facing the guy watching television. My gun is pointed at him and he looks at me with little reaction. I wonder if he is mentally impaired.

'Where is Jackie?' I ask with a firmness that surprises me.

'She not here,' the man answers in a thick Russian accent.

'Don't bullshit me,' I say, wondering if he could be telling the truth.

He grins. 'No bullshit.'

I walk over to him and smash the butt of the gun into the side of his face. Blood flows from his nose. The bleeding is significant and he'll need hospital attention. Even if he is telling the truth, it's satisfying to wipe the smirk from his visage. 'So where is she?'

He wipes away some of the blood with his shirt sleeve. 'Go fuck yourself,' he says, defiant. Obviously Antonovich has instilled either loyalty or fear into him.

I smash the gun into his head, hard. He plops over, unconscious. I search his clothing and find a gun in a side pocket. I remove it and stick it under my trouser belt, at the back. No point in leaving it around to do some harm. I may become a collector of guns, I imagine. Better than collecting stamps as a hobby.

I walk quickly through the place. On this one level, there are three bedrooms, a bathroom, a kitchen and the lounge room I just vacated. Where the hell could anyone hide a person? Just as I'm about to exit the rear door I notice an internal door opposite the lounge. I try the handle but it's locked. I return to the fallen goon, now dripping blood all over the grey sofa, and search for a key. I find a set of keys in his other pocket.

Of the four keys, two are too small for the door. The second key of appropriate size is the last chance as the first one proved useless. I try it. It fits. I push the door open and see steps leading down. I find a light switch and then I see the basement, which appears to be made up as another bedroom. I descend the stairs slowly, the gun to my side. Halfway down I see Jackie lying on a bed in a corner. Her eyes are closed. Her right wrist is shackled to the wall by a chain fitted to handcuffs. I pocket the gun and when I reach the bottom, Jackie opens her eyes. When she recognises me, she beams.

I race over and give her a hug. 'Thank God you're alive. Are you hurt?'

'I'm fine. It's great to see you. How did you find me?'

'I'll tell you later. First let's get you out of here.' I try the smaller keys and one releases her from the cuffs. I take her wrist and massage it.

'There, let's go.'

We begin to move to the stairs when I hear the door shut. I hurry up and find it's been locked. Damn. I should have done the guard more harm – hit him harder or tied him up. I look back and see the disappointment on Jackie's face. I take her hand and lead her to the bed and we both sit. I face her. 'Look I'll get the door open but I want you to stay put until I do.'

'How are you going to do that?'

I produce the gun from my pocket. Her expression is priceless and I'm tempted to take her there and then but getting out urgently is a priority. Who knows how strong Antonovich's army of thugs is? I sneak up the stairs and look at the lock. It's crucial that when I burst through the door I act quickly. I expect the goon is outside waiting with a knife or club or something. I take aim and fire two quick shots at the lock. It breaks and I pull the door open and step out. What I see shocks me. The goon has another pistol and he fires but I return fire and hit him in the middle of the chest. He falls and the pistol slips out of his hand and crashes to the ground with a thud. I check his pulse. He's gone. Dead. Departed. Over.

Only then do I see that his bullet has struck me on my left arm, my non-shooting arm. Jackie has come up and she screams when she sees the blood.

'It's only a scratch,' I say, taking the thug's gun off the floor.

'We'll have to go to a hospital,' she says.

'No, they'll ask too many questions.' I go into a bedroom and rummage through drawers. I find a T-shirt and apply it tightly around the wound.

Jackie looks on, bewildered. 'Are you always this stubborn?'

'Probably, but I'd like you to be my nurse. You should be used to it by now.'

Chapter 35 Friday/Saturday

Jackie is sitting on a kitchen chair, a cup of tea in front of her, still shaking from the recent ordeal. We had taken the Mercedes to North Sydney, parked the car in the street a block away from my Audi, and then we'd driven that to her flat in Bellevue Hill. I'm nursing a scotch, looking down into it, wondering what my next step should be.

'Aren't you going to call the police?' Jackie takes a sip of the hot brew.

'Good idea. I don't want to answer any questions yet so I'll use your landline, if I may.' I place the call to the North Sydney Police Station and inform the desk sergeant that something nasty has happened at the Greenwich address we'd just escaped from. I hang up when he asks who I am.

'What now?' she prods.

'I don't know,' I say, thinking about how best to keep her safe. 'Let me take you to my mother's place until this is over. They know your address and mine so we'll keep a low profile until Sunday when the article is due to come out.'

Jackie gets up without committing. 'I'll take a shower and change,' she says. She walks off towards the bathroom.

Antonovich would have gotten wind of what's happened, I imagine, or he will shortly. At least I have four guns as part of my armoury: my own gun, the one from Nikolai, and two from the dead guy in Lane Cove. I could start a war. But I'm getting ahead of myself. I wonder why it's so important that Antonovich's brother-in-law gets elected. What does Antonovich have to gain? I call Stan and ask him to do some background checks on Magnus Kuklev, the politician, and tell him to call me at any time, day or night. After all I may need to update the article with additional information.

Jackie returns, showered and wearing a fresh outfit as well as carrying a small travel bag. I help her place the luggage into the boot of the car and she tells me she's not happy with this disruption to her life. I apologise but don't know what else to say.

We arrive at my mother's a short time later. Luckily she is still away with her new love interest so we can settle into her place without much fuss. I text my mother to explain what's happening, saying that we need a safe house for a few days.

'I have to call my staff,' Jackie says.

'Of course,' I say, leaving her in peace. I walk into the spare bedroom where I've stayed before and make sure it's set up properly. The prospect of spending the night with Jackie excites me, despite the danger we're both in.

Taking two pistols, I tell Jackie I'll be out for a short time and that she should make herself at home. I kiss her on the lips and waltz out the door, feeling strangely light-headed.

Three and a half hours later I return with groceries and my laptop.

'That took a long time,' she remarks as I empty the bags of goodies.

'Just had to take care of a few things,' I say. To avoid further questioning, I add, 'Why don't you fix us each a drink while I make dinner?' Now, making dinner is a big deal for me. I've cooked stuff for myself but I've never made dinner for any of my previous female friends. So Jackie qualifies as special or at least different, to be given this treatment by me. Yet a number of women have made me dinner. My first real girlfriend – defined, in my terms, as someone I've been in a relationship with for more than a month – asked me to her place when I was just twenty-two. She was twenty-five and seemed very keen on me. She made Wiener Schnitzel, one of my favourites, with potatoes and peas. The relationship lasted almost six months and I was concerned we were headed for the aisle so I had to do a Houdini. My excuse, at least to myself, was that I was far too young to begin a marriage.

'Is a scotch okay?' asks Jackie.

'Absolutely. My mother stocks it for me. She only drinks white wine.'

We sit down to dinner, spaghetti with prawns, garlic and chilli, at eight o'clock. Jackie makes agreeable sounds so I guess I pass the test of being able to provide adequate sustenance. I refill her glass with red wine, which I'd also just purchased. Finished, we sit in the lounge and put on the television like an old married couple.

'Thank you. That was nice,' she says.

'Let's … '

A loud banging on the door disrupts the tranquillity of our evening and my thought process. I jump up, grab a gun and walk to the door. What the hell? Did Antonovich somehow find us? How? I look through the peephole. I can't see anybody. I open the door. Nobody there. I walk a few steps and note a head disappearing around hedges. Are these the teenagers my mother has been telling me about? Troublemakers waking people up? My mother would be too slow to chase them. But I'm not. I move silently around the other side of the hedge and see two youths silently laughing. They don't see me yet. I move closer and tap one on the shoulder. He turns, sees the gun, and freezes. His mate does the same.

'Can I help you?' I say, pointing the pistol at the first youth, a boy of around sixteen.

'No, sir, we were just having some fun. Please don't shoot.'

'Take me to your house,' I order.

They hesitate. I cock the gun. They seem less sure of themselves and I follow them to a house three blocks away. I knock on the door. A man of fifty answers.

'Yes?' he says.

'Do you know these youngsters?' I say, having put the gun in the waistband at the small of my back.

'That's my son Timmy and his mate Arthur.'

I explain the problem my mother and other neighbours have had and suggest he applies discipline and provides stern words to them before the police become involved. The man looks at his son and points his finger at him to go inside the house. He tells Arthur to go home. He thanks me and pleads for me not to call the police as the boys have had previous run-ins with the authorities.

Having dealt with this matter positively, I feel good when I return to Jackie. I take her hand and lead her into the bedroom.

***

It's 4:16 am and I wake with a start, disentangling myself from Jackie who seems to be sound asleep. My article won't appear in any Sunday paper but rather the *Good Weekend* magazine inside the paper or within the *Review* section, I don't know which exactly. Which means it won't appear this weekend but next weekend. What an idiot I've been. The communication with the paper hadn't been clear or I've misunderstood it. I'm not sure which. But it means I need to keep Jackie safe for another week. She shouldn't go to work but she may object. I need to deal with these questions in the cold light of day. I close my eyes again and put my arm over Jackie who hasn't stirred. But my thoughts keep me awake for some time.

At 8 am Jackie puts her lips to my cheek and I wake. 'Ooh, that's rough,' she says smoothing the bristle on my face with the palm of her hand.

I sit up and look at her. Even now she looks beautiful. Am I in love? This is not normally a thought that crosses my mind when I see a woman next to me in the morning. 'Let's shower,' I say.

'Together?'

'Yes, what's the problem?'

'No problem but we're becoming very intimate.'

'That's not bad, is it?'

Jackie grins. 'I didn't say that.'

We saunter into the shower and rub soap over each other then let the strong flow of water wash it away. I kiss her all over when the soap has disappeared and she reciprocates. During this time I think about nothing except what we're doing. But as I dress I realise the fun, for the time being, is over. We have to stay vigilant and also resolve what needs to happen to tackle the problem we face.

Chapter 36 Saturday

While I make eggs on toast, Jackie pours the coffee. She looks wonderful, her face glowing, a far cry from when I encountered her in Antonovich's basement. It's a sunny day promising to be hot and ideal for the beach but that's not what I need to concern myself with. Will Antonovich's network have the ability to carry out a search for us throughout the Eastern suburbs? I guess we could always travel elsewhere but that idea holds no appeal.

'Are you thinking about going to the hair salon?' I ask.

'I should. What do you think?'

I finalise the breakfast and set the plates down and we sit on stools opposite each other at the kitchen island. 'I don't think it's wise. Not until this whole business with Antonovich is over.'

Jackie is hungry and is digging into her breakfast with gusto. 'When will that be?'

'I don't know but I hope publishing … '

My sentence is interrupted by the phone. I see that it's none other than my intrepid researcher, Stan. 'Sorry, I need to take this.' I speak into my phone facing away from Jackie. 'Yes, Stan.'

'Good morning. Can you talk?'

'Sure.'

'Antonovich's brother-in-law, Kuklev, should he be elected, will have pull with the local council.'

'Why is that?'

'Well,' he says, pausing, 'seems that the local council has a member who has bet on Kuklev to lose. If he wins, the local member will step down, which will change the balance of power.'

Intrigued, I drink some coffee and look at Jackie who has now finished her eggs on toast. 'So?'

'The voice against extra infrastructure spend will have gone. That member, David Granger, has fought for ages to ensure local places of interest are not torn down so that developers can erect blocks of high-rise apartments. Antonovich's company will probably get the nod for contracts which will arise from his brother-in-law's promise of significant infrastructure in his electorate.'

'So Antonovich stands to gain millions?'

'Looks like it.'

'Hmm,' I say, 'I understand why he needs his relative in government – money. Typical. I'm sure this brother-in-law, Kuklev or whatever his name is, will benefit too. Politicians and businessmen have had connections throughout history.'

'Yes. Will you make changes to the article?'

'Absolutely. Have you confirmed that Jay is the leaker?'

'We have. He'll be dismissed once this whole matter is done. He has your fake article so he will pass that information on to Antonovich.'

'Good. So he'll alert Antonovich that the new piece will be in line with his suggestions. '

'We'll publish your amended story next weekend. Maxine asks that you send it to us by Tuesday at 5 pm.'

'Will do,' I say, and finish the call. I turn back to Jackie and tell her what's transpired.

'So in a week, this situation will have resolved itself?'

'I expect so.'

'Why can't we report the kidnapping?'

'Because I shot that guy, you know – where you were held. And I have a plan for Antonovich, so talking to the police now will only cloud matters,' I say, taking her hand. 'Please just bear with me for the week.'

Jackie gazes at me affectionately. 'Okay. I'll call the salon and say I'll be on leave for a while.'

At that moment the door opens and my mother walks in. When she sees me, she beams. 'What an unexpected delight, Nick.' She kisses me on the cheek then notices Jackie.

'Mum, meet Jackie,' I say.

'Hello, Jackie. Nice to meet you.' Then she turns back to me. 'Why are you here, Nick, and not at your place?'

'It's complicated. Sit down and have a cup of coffee and I'll fill you in.'

Over the next ten minutes I explain in summary form what's happened and what's happening. 'That's about the size of it,' I say, finishing my story.

'You're both welcome to stay as long as you want. It'll be nice to have company.' She looks at Jackie, who thanks her.

'Let me give you a tour of the place,' says Mother, who takes Jackie along. 'We'll let Nick do his work.'

At 6 pm I stop tinkering with the article. I've rearranged it, added to it and I'm ready for a break. The women are out, shopping probably. I asked them to avoid Bondi Junction in case Antonovich or his men are searching for Jackie. I go to the fridge and take out a bottle of cold water. It's been hot and I wonder how the lads are going at cricket. I had to say I was unavailable again. I'm really keen to get a hit but this job needs to take priority. Responsible me. I hate myself sometimes doing the right thing always, well mostly. I wonder whether shooting the guy who was guarding Jackie was the right thing to do. I would rather have been able to escape without killing him but I had no time to consider options. After all it was self-defence. He would have killed me had I not fired.

I get a call from mum who invites me to join her, her new man Brian, and Jackie for dinner at a Mosman restaurant. I figure it should be safe enough and accept.

***

191

Brian Wentworth is a short man, about five foot six, with thick brown hair and sparkling eyes. He's dressed in cream slacks, a light green shirt and a tan jacket. He rises and shakes my hand when I approach their table. 'I've heard a lot about you,' he says.

'Nice to meet you. I see you've met my girlfriend Jackie.'

'Oh yes, would you like a glass of champagne?' he says as Jackie gives me a look suggesting I should ask her first before offering her up as mine.

'Sounds good,' I say as I sit next to Jackie and give her a pat on her thigh. 'What have you and Mother been up to this afternoon?'

'That's between us girls,' Mother interrupts.

'Naturally,' I say, not wanting to cause waves. 'I hear you're a retired gentleman, Brian.'

'Sort of. I keep my hand in with the occasional consultancy.'

I look bemused and he adds, 'I'm a chartered accountant by profession and I advise companies and individuals on a variety of matters. Takeovers, mergers, tax and a host of minor accounting treatments.'

'Have you heard of a fellow called Karlos Antonovich?'

'As a matter of fact I have. He owns a construction company. He's sleazy to say the least. I'd keep well away from him, if I were you.'

'Right,' I say, wondering whether to explore this further but deciding to say no more. You can never tell who's trustworthy and as I don't know Brian there's no point in revealing more. When I'd told Mother our story I hadn't mentioned names, and I figure it's best for all concerned that I keep the details to myself. 'I'm hungry. What looks good?'

'Everything,' says Jackie. 'It all sounds tasty.'

I know Jackie likes her food and she loves to cook. I'm pleased that Mum and Brian, who seems like a decent guy, invited her along. And it appears that Mum has taken to Jackie, which I'm also happy about. So everything is looking positive: a great assignment, which could bring more work from Maxine's paper, Mum with a new man, and Jackie who is warming to me. I study the menu.

As I place the menu on the table, I see Karlos Antonovich enter the restaurant with a woman who is not his wife. He sees me and stares. He knows that Jackie is no longer leverage. I hope he won't start anything in here. I watch while he and his attractive young floozy are taken to their seats not far from us.

'Do you actually know Antonovich?' I ask Brian, who's opposite me.

'Well … as I recall, I met him here. It's one of his haunts.'

I see. The Bathers Pavilion Restaurant at Balmoral Beach, a popular tourist part of Mosman, is a classy joint, so I'm not surprised Antonovich likes to come here. It's not too far from his home but far enough away for him to dine with his mistress.

As we order our meals my mind is on the man in the corner about three tables away. Now that he's seen us I'm worried he might attempt to hurt or threaten my mother as well as my lover. He's a crook and a thug and he thinks he can muscle his way into millions of dollars simply by lying and cheating. I hate his kind and I'm going to make his life hell. But the risk is that he'll do the same to my life.

As we eat and chat I remain fairly quiet, contemplating what I can do to ensure the safety of my loved ones. Jackie hasn't reacted when she looked across at the couple so I imagine Antonovich wasn't in the group of men who ambushed her or else he was covered up with a hood or a ski mask. But I suspect he had his henchmen do the job. I recall her story of the kidnapping. She'd been surprised in the car park coming home from work by suddenly feeling a hand over her face and a knife pointed under her throat. Told not to make a sound, she was forced into the backseat of a vehicle, blindfolded and bound while one man sat beside her and another drove. She said she hadn't seen the faces of her attackers. She was taken to the basement, and food was supplied by a hooded captor. The story made my blood boil.

After tasting my main course I excuse myself and make my way to the bathroom. I have a plan. As I walk back, I go to Antonovich's table.

Chapter 37 Saturday/Sunday

'Mr Hunter, how nice to see you again,' Antonovich says.

I look at him and say, 'Yes, I didn't know you frequented this part of town.'

'I know most of the quality restaurants around the place,' he says, looking self-satisfied.

'And you're not going to introduce your lovely companion?' I watch his reaction, which is smooth, without a hint of anxiety.

'Pardon my manners,' he says. Then, gesturing to the tall magnificent blonde, he adds, 'This is Sophia, a friend.'

'Pleased to meet you,' I say, extending a hand, which she ignores, simply nodding. I wonder whether she's an escort or whether he actually knows her. Nothing would surprise me.

'I see you're with family,' he says.

'Very observant,' I say, tempted to break a glass and spear it into his face. The subtle threat makes me want to be unpleasant but I hold fire. 'I should get back.'

Sophia gets up and walks away, presumably to the ladies. Perhaps she was feeling exposed.

'Sit down and have a drink,' Antonovich orders.

I sit down by pulling a chair across from another table, not wanting to upset Sophia. I don't expect him to be carrying a concealed gun but I'm curious. What is he going to propose? He turns and signals the waiter and asks for another wine glass. As the waiter pours me a white wine, I ask, 'What's your wife up to tonight? Television or seeing friends?'

'I'm not amused. You broke into my home. You'll pay for that.'

'And kidnapping is acceptable?'

He is barely able to contain his anger, his facial features flushed. I wonder whether he is going to lose his temper. The restaurant is about three-quarters full now and patrons are still arriving. If he makes a scene the manager may call the police, something I wouldn't like but I'd take it in my stride. I have less to lose than he does.

'Once the promised article appears in the newspaper as required, the problems your family faces go away. But let me warn you that if you trespass on my properties again, you will not like the consequences.'

I stand up and in the process I knock the table. The glass of wine falls and the contents spill. Sophia arrives and she yelps like a dog. Wait staff converge and in the confusion a knife falls to the ground. I pick it up and go back to my table. I place the knife in a napkin and sit down.

'What were you doing at that table?' my mother asks with Jackie looking on.

'I was just having a chat with a business colleague,' I say.

We finish the dinner and I try to contribute to the conversation but my heart is not in it. Jackie and I say goodnight to Brian and my mother who will stay over at his place. Once Jackie is in my car, she asks about the man I spoke with.

'That was the man who kidnapped you. Well, his thugs did the work but he ordered the job.'

'Jesus. Why did you talk to him?' Jackie says in a high-pitched voice.

'I needed to clarify a few things,' I explain. 'He wants something and I need to be patient a little longer. Just go with it for now. Please.' I take her hand and look into her eyes. 'You'll be fine.'

'Okay,' she says.

As we drive back to Bellevue Hill, Jackie asks, 'Why did you take a napkin from the restaurant?'

'Souvenir.'

'You're a strange man.'

'So I've been told.'

That night the sex is particularly spirited. Whether it's the prospect of new dangers or because the food and drink are agreeable, I don't know. All I care about now is enjoying Jackie. I fall asleep almost immediately afterwards.

I wake early. Jackie is fast asleep. I sneak out of the house and drive off, down to New South Head Road, across the bridge and up the Pacific Highway. At this time of day on a Sunday there is little traffic. The day comes with a clear blue sky and everything seems peaceful. I have one more thing to do before I can relax and let things take their course. I know that plans don't always work out but at least I can be proactive and try to arrange matters to go my way. Letting things work themselves out is generally a risky business. I arrive at the planned location and look about. The entire exercise, including the travel, is over in a little more than an hour. I bring croissants home for breakfast. Jackie is towelling her hair so she's excited to see me. We embrace and enjoy coffee with what I've brought.

'Lovely day for the beach,' I say.

'It is. Where should we go?'

My phone disturbs the atmosphere. I can't believe it. It's Claire. I walk outside to talk without being overheard. 'Hello,' I say, keeping my voice neutral.

'Hi Nick, I have a problem.'

So do I, I almost say. But I keep quiet and wait for more.

'Nick, are you there?'

'Of course, sorry. I'm waiting to hear about your problem,' I say.

'I can't, not over the phone. Can you come over?'

Is she being harassed by criminals too? What could be so urgent? I'm about to reply when I hear her sob. I don't like women crying. 'Okay, I'll pop over.' Frustrated and annoyed, I explain the situation to Jackie who is understanding and tells me to go, to sort it out.

When Claire opens the door, I note an alarmed expression on her face. Then she recognises me and starts to cry again. She rushes into my arms and I don't know what to do. After a moment she disengages herself and walks into her dingy flat. I follow, wondering what's going on. When she turns around again she wipes tears from her cheeks and then I notice a bruise.

'What happened to you?' I say, pointing to the bruise on the side of her right cheek, which had been partially covered by hair when I'd greeted her.

'He hit me.'

'Who hit you?'

'Never mind. At least you came. I want you back.'

I loathe this kind of situation. I could be brutal and tell her I'm not interested but she looks so pathetic that I'll feel miserable if I do it. I should have asked Jackie to call so I have an excuse to leave in a hurry. So I change tack. 'Tell me who hurt you.'

'My brother,' she says sheepishly.

'Why, an argument?'

She takes me by the hand and sits me down on a tacky sofa, which must have been second hand when acquired by Claire or her flatmate, who isn't in. She looks me in the eye and says, 'There's something I never told you.'

'Yes,' I say, wondering what kind of explanation she might have to lure me here. I now understand that the whole weeping saga is a ploy.

'My brother and I are more than, you know … '

'Sorry, I don't know.'

'We're also lovers.'

I'm not sure how to handle this news. Of course, it's really none of my business. 'Is that why you couldn't be contacted on your travels?'

'Partly, but we were also in isolated places, as I told you.'

I don't know whether to believe her. 'So if he hits you, why don't you break it off with him?' This sounds logical to me and I can't imagine an argument that could refute this.

'It's complicated,' she says, keeping her eyes on the floor.

'How complicated could it be? Tell him to clear off or you'll expose him.'

'I couldn't do that,' she says, screwing up her lips.

'Why?' I say, unable to comprehend her stupidity. To think I was involved with a woman so emotionally bankrupt staggers me. Why couldn't I see something was amiss?

'It's a family thing,' she says.

'What's that mean? Your parents know?'

'Yes, but they're part of it.'

'What – they're involved too?' I laugh. This must be some story she's making up. She probably needs professional help.

She says in a matter-of-fact voice, 'Yes. My father has had sex with me, and my brother has had sex with my mother, and we've all done it together in one big bed.'

'You're joking,' I say.

'All right, I am. My brother and I have done it since we were teenagers.'

'And your parents?'

'They probably know. I don't know for sure but I think so.'

What a freak show. I don't know whether to believe it but somehow I do. Her crying has stopped and she looks at me to see whether there is understanding and sympathy. 'I don't know how I can help you.'

'I want you back. You've always treated me well and I want to get away from him and these regular family holidays.'

So I'm a convenience. Somebody to let her escape from the clutches of her weird family. 'Look I'd be happy to if I loved you but I don't.'

She looks as though she's about to burst into tears. I stand up and go towards the door. There I turn around and say. 'I can recommend someone who may be able to help you through this. Do you want me to write it down for you?'

'No, bugger off.'

I leave. It's all too much for me. However as I drive back to my mother's place, I imagine that Claire's account would make a good story. It also makes me think that, like everyone, there must be dirt to uncover with Antonovich and it might be useful to obtain any dirty secrets in the event he makes further threats on either Jackie or Mum.

Buoyed by this I make a mental list of what needs to be done.

Chapter 38 Monday

When I rub my eyes awake and check the time, nearly seven o'clock, I turn to find Jackie missing. Probably in the bathroom, I figure. I stretch. It takes me a moment to get familiar again with the fact I'm staying in my mother's spare room. Sliding out of bed, I do fifty push-ups and then wander to the bathroom. I recall the night before when Jackie and I had a modest dinner with her cooking in Mum's kitchen. The outcome, lamb chops and vegetables, was delicious. During dinner I explained what Claire wanted and Jackie was speechless when I told her of my former girlfriend's story of incest with her brother. After cleaning up, we'd sat down in the living room and watched a film on Foxtel. During the movie, we continued talking and I informed Jackie of my plan to find some dirt on Antonovich.

'What about his mistress from the Bathers Pavilion?' she'd said.

'There's probably more to uncover,' I'd responded.

The discussion on that topic had ended there and we'd enjoyed the rest of the evening, unconcerned about the world beyond the four walls we were in.

Now, I sit at the breakfast island after my shower realising that Jackie isn't anywhere inside, and wondering where she could be. Surely she hasn't gone to work? I switch on the television to see what's happening in the world. As I prepare to make coffee, Jackie comes in and places croissants and pastries on the kitchen island. 'I needed to stretch my legs so I bought some stuff at the local bakery,' she says.

'Great,' I say. 'I was debating what to have for breakfast.'

I make coffee and we have our breakfast in relative silence as we view News Breakfast on the ABC. A breaking news story holds my attention. The reporter outside a home in McMahons Point talks while the pictures reveal that a man who looks like Karlos Antonovich is being escorted out of his house. 'The police today have arrested a prominent Sydney businessman for murder. It is understood a tip-off has helped them find a pistol used in the murder of a Lane Cove man.'

'Aha,' I say. 'Finally they've found it.'

'Were you the tip-off?'

'Yes. I used the same trick Antonovich used to disguise his voice, and I told the police where I dumped the gun and I guess it must be registered in his name.'

'Will that be enough to convict him?'

'No, but I also transferred his fingerprints from the knife I took at the restaurant to the gun used to kill the guy guarding you in that Lane Cove house.'

Jackie looks admiringly at me, 'You have been busy.'

'He'll get lawyers to challenge everything but it'll slow him down. At least it'll take his mind off us for a while.'

'You've effectively framed him for a murder he didn't commit?'

I finish my first cup of coffee. 'If you consider the murder of Don Murphy and your kidnapping are going unpunished, I figure he deserves all he gets, although I suspect he'll get off.'

Jackie snuggles up to me. 'Remind me not to get into your bad books.'

I kiss her neck. 'I can't ever see that happening.'

'So do you think we can return home?'

I ponder the question. As much as I'd like to make absolutely certain that Jackie remains safe, it's impractical to live hidden away. 'Probably.' I gaze into her eyes. 'I have to admit though that it's great to have you so close each day.'

'It was good to see how we interacted, living together for a few days, I must admit. It's been very enjoyable but I have to earn a living. I'm not independently wealthy like some.'

I realise she's having a dig at me but I don't take the bait. Instead, I kiss her on the lips, but she's not tempted to go further.

We agree to clean up then return to our respective homes. I drive Jackie to her place. We kiss goodbye and I suggest we meet again on Friday night for dinner at a favourite restaurant of hers. I arrive home mid-morning and check my mail. I also see what I have in the fridge and draw up a list of groceries and other household items to buy. On my way to the shops I stop in at my regular café and note that Julie is working.

'Haven't seen you for a few days,' she says when she places the cappuccino I ordered on the table. 'Been away?'

'You could say that. And you? Sorted out your boyfriend problems?'

'Not really, but I'm not worried. My best friend Amy and I have been enjoying time together.'

'That's great. Things often work out for the best if you let time do the work.' I can't believe I said that but for some people it takes an event to alter their habits, and then good things arise. Still, I'm determined to continue with my investigation into Antonovich.

I complete my shopping and at home I settle down to check out my Russian friend. I find his Facebook page and examine it. It shows he's from Saint Petersburg, a port city on the Baltic Sea in Russia, and that he studied at the University of New South Wales. I look at his list of friends and scribble interesting looking names on a piece of paper. I intend to check out some of these on their Facebook accounts. Additionally, I will consider contacting a sample of them for further information. It seems that Antonovich likes opera, snow skiing and cards.

One name in particular is of interest. I recognise it from accounts in the newspaper in connection with a Sydney council. This man is a councillor and may have given Antonovich special treatment. I google news about this issue and find that the council has been exposed as potentially corrupt. The article contended that the council had been involved in defending legal proceedings against it in relation to giving preferential consideration to a suspected Russian criminal but nothing had eventuated. The hearing had run into a dead end when Antonovich denied any wrong doing in connection with the transformation of a building. He had been accused of building an apartment block which contained unapproved alterations, turning many two-bedroom flats into three-bedroom flats and thereby creating safety hazards. The matter was somehow never followed up.

So Antonovich is dirty, no question about it. I feel no remorse about what I have done to have him arrested. I bet he has become financially enriched by his dealings in many shady projects and I wouldn't be surprised if he was also involved in stand-over tactics and possibly manipulation of a variety of regulations. But to prove what I suspect would be difficult if the authorities had not been able to pin anything on him.

It is nearly dinnertime when I finish my research. Should I alter my article? I doubt it would make any difference. The piece might be delayed because of the extra fact checking. No, it's enough that I know. I get up and stretch. I need to take a walk. My head will explode if I continue to read any more articles about allegations of corrupt business dealings.

As I walk down the street my mother calls to say she has returned home and is wondering why Jackie and I have gone. When I explain she says she understands but also says that I should bring Jackie over for a Sunday lunch in a couple of weeks. She says she likes Jackie and thinks she would be good for me. Generally a mother's approval of a girlfriend is a kiss of death for the relationship but in this instance I don't react. Jackie would be good for me, I believe. I click off and continue my stroll.

As I get to New South Head Road I experience hunger pangs and decide to have a pizza at Grandfather's Moustache. I review the menu and settle on the Seafood Pizza and a coffee, a flat white for a change. I want to think things through. What is the value of trying to contact any of Antonovich's friends? I know enough to realise he is crooked but also that he has friends in high places who will help him if he's in trouble. They won't reveal anything more incriminating unless I have some leverage. And I don't have the time to carry out such research. I will await the reaction to my weekend piece. After my meal I step back outside and wonder what Jackie is doing. I'm tempted to call her but I imagine she's had enough of me for now. I don't want to come across as needy.

As I get to the door of my apartment I sense something is amiss. But I can't put my finger on it. It's nothing tangible except for something as silly as a whiff of aftershave in the air. Surely I'm imagining things. I open up and switch on the light. Then I realise that's somebody's been here. I'd left my laptop cover up and now it's down. Strange. Am I dreaming? Have I lost my memory again? I walk over to my laptop and open it. I'm sure I'd signed off and it would require somebody to crack my password to get inside to the contents.

'Don't move,' a voice says, adding, 'Hands up and put them on your head.'

I do as requested. The voice is behind me. The person must have been hiding in the bathroom. I have one on this level as well as an en suite on the bedroom level. I'm not going to speak. Let him do the running.

'Turn around real slow and keep the hands on your head.'

As I comply I see that the man who has spoken has a gun point-ed at me. He is accompanied by my old friend, Nikolai, his Ginger Beard still full on his face. Obviously he doesn't believe in trimming it.

'How can I help you gentlemen?' I ask. The guys are standing a few metres away, too far for me to attempt any kicks or punches.

The voice answers. He is a tall slender man dressed in jeans and a T-shirt. 'You shot our colleague and I want you to admit it. You will explain this to the police in a recording that we will make. Understood?'

Nikolai is smiling. He is no doubt pleased that he'll have the last laugh. I'm not sure how they expect the police to believe a recorded message. Is it purely to provide doubt as to the guilt of Antonovich who has communicated to his underlings and suggested this crazy idea? Of course they may get me to describe details as they see it but then it would be unbelievable. 'I understand. But if I record something under duress it won't stand up in court.'

'Our boss will get bail and when the article is released next weekend, he won't care anymore because you will be dead by your own hand.'

'Why don't you take me to a police station so I can provide a statement?'

'Very funny.' The man with the gun says. 'You think this is a joke. Sit in the armchair.' He turns to his companion. 'Nikolai, start the phone video when I say, okay?'

'Okay, Gus,' he responds.

'I have written what you are going to say on here,' Gus says. He passes an A4-sized page of printer paper to me.

I read it and almost laugh but, given that I detected a lacking of any sense of humour in the tall man, I desist. 'What if I refuse?'

'We know you rescued a woman from our Lane Cove place so we can take her again. Is that what you want?'

Will this nightmare ever stop? 'All right, I'll go along with what you want.' Apparently I'm to explain the purpose of my confession, then describe in detail how I killed Nikolai's mate without mentioning the kidnapping. Neat. I realise I have to think on my feet. I recall where I've kept my guns. My own gun is in the bedroom and the one I took from Nikolai is in my desk drawer. Have they found it, I wonder, as I prepare myself for the job at hand.

'Right,' Gus says, 'speak and don't look at the notes.' He looks at Nikolai, 'Begin the video.'

'My name is Nick Hunter and I'm responsible for the death of Alexei Minayev, the man shot in Lane Cove. I'm making this confession because I don't want to see an innocent man charged for this crime. To confirm that I am the man who did this … '

My phone rings. 'Should I get that?' I say.

Gus, the tall streak of misery slouching slightly, looks annoyed. He waits then says, 'Answer but be careful what you say.' To Nikolai he says, 'We'll have to start again.'

I take the phone out of my pocket and look at the screen. It's Maxine.

'Hi,' I say, 'Nick Hunter here.'

'I know who it is,' Maxine says. 'Can you talk?'

'Not really. What do you want?'

'You don't sound like yourself. Are you okay?'

'No. I need to finish my article,' I say hoping Maxine realises something is wrong.

'Someone's there?'

'Yes.'

'Are you in danger?'

'Absolutely.'

'Stay calm, I'll get help.' Maxine hangs up.

I continue talking, hoping to delay the inevitable. I have a premonition that as soon as I've delivered my confession Gus and Nikolai will get rid of me somehow – unpleasantly, no doubt. Antonovich may have told his followers that the article has been completed and that he's satisfied with the version he saw thanks to the efforts of his newspaper insider. This means I'm expendable and the only matter to be resolved for the Russian kingpin is getting out of custody. I eventually hang up when Gus waves his gun at me.

'Sit down. Give me your phone,' Gus says. I toss it to him and he catches it. 'Now start again and don't let anything interrupt the recording.'

I view the piece of paper again and smile at the thugs. 'Just checking the script,' I say. I don't know what to do to delay this or whether in fact Maxine can convince somebody to rescue me. When they shoot me, will my life flood before my eyes? What have I done so far? I've lived a fairly interesting life without the childhood trauma and tragedies that many of the people I know have endured. Ross, a schoolmate, had a mother with ovarian cancer and a father in a wheelchair. Randy, a former work colleague, had been beaten growing up. Cindy, a friend of an early girlfriend, grew up with no father and poverty. So I can't complain but I have a lot of living to do. And there's Jackie, someone I'd like to begin a joint life with.

'Right,' I say. 'As before?'

'Yes, exactly like that and explain what happened, that you shot Alexei when you saw him.'

'In self-defence?'

Gus is getting irritated. 'I don't care but make it sound good. And nothing about a kidnapping. Got it?'

'Of course,' I say. I begin as before and my mind is struggling with finding a way out of this situation. I look at Nikolai who is holding the iPhone steady. Occasionally he twists his face, the Ginger Beard moving, as though he has a twitch. Gus is holding his pistol but has loosened his arm, which is no longer positioned high and straight, but lower, in a more relaxed pose. Towards the end of the confession but before mentioning shooting Alexei, I say, 'Then I saw this man in the lounge holding a gun at me and I had no choice. Antonovich's underling made … '

'Stop!' Gus shouts. 'What are you doing? That's not what you say.'

Nikolai walks towards me and raises his hand to smack me. I wait until the last moment then use my feet to push him away. A shot sounds and I realise Gus has pulled the trigger but the bullet hits Nikolai in the back. I roll off the armchair and rush towards my desk. Other shots ring out but they zing past me. I open the desk drawer and, using it as cover, scramble around, now holding my gun. Gus is out of sight but as he emerges I fire and hit him, as the bullet doesn't sound like it's gone into the wall, but when he screams I realise I've only winged him. He scurries out of sight.

Surely the noise has alerted somebody, hopefully somebody nearby. Gunshots – which are not normal in this quiet suburb and es-

207

pecially in this conservative location – are creating damage to my flat. I wait but nothing happens. No door knocks, no police, no reappearance of Gus. I hold the gun steady. Has Nikolai been killed or is he simply wounded? I poke my head around the corner. A shot rings out and I'm trapped. Obviously Gus is still about.

'Come out,' he calls. 'You will die unless you surrender now.'

'Are you more stupid than you look?' I say, wondering how this insult will be received.

I don't have long to wait. Gus charges around the corner, firing indiscriminately. I return fire and this time he goes down. Then I collapse.

Chapter 39 Tuesday

I hear voices but can't quite make them out. My eyes are closed and I feel drowsy. Where am I? All I recall is a sharp pain then I sort of blacked out. The events slowly come back. A gunfight. But not at the OK Corral – instead, in my apartment. I wonder whether I'm insured for damage caused by the bullets, which are now embedded in the walls throughout my place.

A third voice interrupts my thoughts but this one is louder. 'He should wake soon, once the anaesthetic has worn off. Why don't you go down and have a cup of tea?'

It seems that I'm not at my apartment.

'Should we?' asks my mother in a louder voice.

'I'll stay. You go if you want,' Jackie says.

I try to open my eyes but I can't. I try to speak but nothing comes out. I'll have to be patient. I must be in a hospital as I now get the sense things are sticking out of me. Gadgets are stuck in my arms and a tube seems to be in my mouth. I return to sleep.

Later, I'm not sure how much later, I wake, and this time I can open my eyes. The breathing thing has been removed so my mouth is free again. I see I'm in a bed with rails around the sides. I'm in a room that is pristine white. Two smiling faces emerge. My mother says, 'Nick, how do you feel?'

'I feel odd, like I've been to hell and back. What happened?'

'Hello there,' Jackie says. 'Thank God you're okay. You've been shot and the operation removed the bullet.'

'You're very lucky,' mum says. 'Help arrived quickly.'

I guess I need to find out the specifics in due course but it seems Maxine got someone to get to my place quickly enough. Seeing Jackie and Mum's beaming faces cheers me up more than they can imagine. I smile and play at being submissive. There's nothing I can do at the moment with bandages around my midsection.

A nurse comes in, shooing my visitors aside. She gives me tablets to swallow, explaining that they're painkillers. Surely a few glasses of scotch would be just as effective and far more enjoyable. She also tells me that I need to rest and that visitors can come back the next day. Both Jackie and Mum look sullen as they say goodbye and leave.

'You'll see them again,' the nurse says. She's a sturdy woman in her mid-forties. 'The doctor will be in to see you in the next hour and he won't like people being about.'

'Oh,' I say, not knowing whether this was the doctor's wish or the nurse's. But I don't care as I drift off to sleep.

I awake again when the doctor visits to explain what happened on the operating table. He says that all the fragments of the bullet that hit me had been removed, and remarks on how lucky I am that nothing had threatened a major organ. I almost faint listening to the details. I can happily see killings and other tragedies on the screen but in real life I'm squeamish when it comes to seeing blood. After telling me he's happy with my condition, he informs me he'll pop in again tomorrow to check on my progress. He's a no-nonsense middle-aged man, a short fellow with curly hair and round -rimmed glasses.

'How long do I need to stay here?' I ask.

'In a hurry are we?' he replies.

'I have things to do,' I say, knowing how lame that sounds. What I don't say is that I hate hospitals and I'd like to see Jackie at home where we can cuddle. I doubt I'll be any good in bed for a few days.

'Don't we all,' he says, not sympathetic in the least. 'You need to stay here until I'm certain there'll be no infection from the wound.' He goes and I see the white coat flapping against his lean body.

I must have fallen asleep again as I wake at the sound of the nurse's voice. I open my eyes to see her angular white face peering at me. She is unsmiling and says, 'You have visitors – the police. I've told them not to keep you up for long.' She disappears.

The police! I shouldn't be surprised but I am. I lever myself into a reclining position so that I can see them properly. A well-built man of medium height in a worn grey suit is accompanied by a shorter woman in uniform. He's around forty and the woman is in her twenties.

'I'm DS Daniels and this is DC O'Keefe. How are you feeling, Mr Hunter?'

'All things considered, I feel okay,' I say.

'You're alive at least,' Daniels says. He scratches his chin. 'Can you tell us what happened?'

'I blacked out.'

DC O'Keefe looks on but I notice a slight grin on her face. She is a redhead with small freckles on her otherwise pale white face. Probably of Irish descent, I imagine.

Daniels responds, 'Tell us what happened up until that point.' He nods to O'Keefe who pulls out a notepad and pen.

I run through the details from when I arrived home, explaining how the two intruders wanted me to make a statement that they were filming, and how I got an opportunity to kick at Nikolai until I scrambled to my desk and shot at Gus. I didn't reveal anything relating to the Lane Cove murder.

'Why did they want to record a statement from you?'

'They wanted to have their boss freed from custody, a Mr Antonovich.'

'Really,' Daniels says, looking sceptical. 'Why would they ask you for a statement?'

I have to be careful here. I can't admit to being in the Lane Cove house yet I need to say something that is plausible. 'I'm a freelance journalist and I received information from a source about corruption in government. Mr Antonovich has tried to pressure me into writing an article favourable to himself as he stands to gain financially should his brother-in-law, a Mr Kuklev, be elected in an upcoming by-election.'

'How exactly would an article favour one individual?'

'By reporting something that would harm the chances of the Liberal Party candidate, the one who's standing against Mr Kuklev. This may allow Antonovich to win certain contracts to develop infrastructure in that electorate.'

'I see. But why would he pressure you to admit something detrimental to yourself?'

'I don't know. You'll have to ask him.'

Daniels looks thoughtful. He can't quite make sense of it. 'So if you're going to write something like that, why choose you to confess to a crime to get Antonovich off?'

I peer at his partner who is preoccupied, jotting down notes, and wonder why I'm being quizzed so thoroughly. 'He wants to level blame on someone besides himself. My guess is that he knows I've written the piece and he doesn't have to keep me sweet, and I suspect his henchmen were going to dispose of me after the confession was recorded.'

Daniels seems happier with this explanation. 'Okay. In any case, the two men in the flat, both dead, have been under surveillance for some time. They're scum so in one sense you did us a favour.'

I smile. I've said enough. Good to know I've done a public service.

The detectives turn to go. At the door Daniels stops, looks back and asks, 'By the way, do you have a licence for the gun you used?'

'Yes detective, I do. I bought a pistol for training purposes before leaving for Russia.' I close my eyes, relieved this nightmare is over. Someone saved me from bleeding out, and I have Maxine to thank for getting things moving fast.

In the evening I have another visitor. Jackie brings me a coffee and some books to read.

'You are wonderful,' I say, taking the three novels. 'Real coffee. I've missed it.'

'Thought it must be boring watching the television with limited

212

channels,' she says, taking my hand.

'I haven't watched much. I've slept a lot, though,' I say, looking more closely at Jackie's beautiful face. 'I like your hair.'

'Well I am a hairdresser, and I get it done regularly and for no cost.'

'Perks of the business?'

'Yes. And what are your perks as a journalist? Beatings, hostility and bullets to the body?'

'Never thought of it that way but I'd frame it differently, more like unintended consequences.'

'Perhaps you should take on a different profession, one which is less hazardous.' Jackie moves away, grabs a chair and sits next to the bed. I elevate the bed slightly so I can see her better.

'What do you suggest?'

'I'm only kidding. I doubt you could live without the intrigue of dangerous investigations. What's going to happen now? Are you safe?'

I consider this. I don't want to scare her by admitting I don't know. There is a possibility that Antonovich has more goons about, but given that I've effectively done away with three of them I don't think they'll came around with Antonovich still in custody. However until Antonovich is convicted and sent to prison I can't be sure of anything. I say, 'I think we're safe. I don't want you to worry.'

'Well, I … '

At that moment Jasmine walks in. She's looking at me, smiling, and then sees Jackie and her smile vanishes, replaced by an expression that can almost be described as a scowl. She looks glamorous in a fitted white blouse and a dark skirt, short and also very tight fitting, accentuating her shapely legs. Her hair is piled on top of her head in a bun and she could easily pass for a senior executive in a fashion house.

Jackie peers at Jasmine and again the look is unfriendly. I imagine them standing toe to toe then regarding each other carefully before starting a catfight, engaging in physicality, pulling hair and rolling around the floor. My blood pressure is probably spiking and I trust the nurse will rescue me before my heart fails. But I calm as I see them saying nice things to each other. Crisis averted.

'How do you know Nick?' Jackie asks.

Jasmine pulls up a chair and faces Jackie, who is now facing her. I thought I was meant to be the centre of attention. Jasmine says, 'I was a maid of honour at a wedding and Nick was the best man.'

'Of course. Nick's told me he had a great time at the wedding.'

'So did I. It was fun.'

Jackie stands. 'I need to go. I'm sure you two have a lot of catching up to do.' She gives me a kiss and waves goodbye.

'See you,' I say meekly, not sure what is going to happen.

Jasmine turns to me. 'Who's she?'

Chapter 40 Saturday

I'm back at home. The wound has been dressed again and it feels much better. I get out of bed but dare not do any exercises. I shower as best I can and look in the mirror. My beard has grown over these past few days and I'm inclined to let it continue. I've spooked all my current girlfriends so it won't matter if I look a bit scruffy. I ended up telling Jasmine I wouldn't be seeing her anymore and that Jackie was my girlfriend. Jasmine accepted the news in good grace, which restored my faith in women. But since then I've not heard from Jackie, which has damaged my assessment. Only Mother came to see me after Jasmine's visit.

I feel good and wander down to Rose Bay to buy the weekend paper, which carries my piece because it was considered more appropriate than having it shown in the Sunday edition. I pop into my usual cafe and order a large cappuccino. Julie approaches after a few minutes. 'I haven't seen you for days. What's happened?'

I push the *Sydney Morning Herald* to the side while she places my large mug of coffee in front of me. 'I ran into some trouble but it's sorted now. And you? Any leads on a new boyfriend?'

'I met somebody last night at a club so who knows.' Julie stands up straight. She is tall and slender. Despite my near death experience, it seems I haven't lost my appreciation of feminine beauty.

'Great. Hope it works out. He's not a journo, is he?'

'No, an accountant.'

'That's promising. Keep away from journalists, though. I've lost all my girlfriends.'

'You're pulling my leg.' She saunters off to do more service.

I open the section in the paper that carries my piece. I read it to make sure no radical changes have occurred. I'm pleased. It shows Antonovich in a bad light and implies he's responsible for unsolved crimes, including murder, but without saying he's guilty of anything specific. Just the tone I wanted. Just enough to scare people off his association with political friends. I savour my coffee. I may be without a woman but I have written something I'm proud of.

Finished, I wave adieu to Julie and walk out into the sunshine. It looks like it's going to be a warm pleasant day, a day for sport. I wonder whether I can resume cricket next Saturday. I should check with the hospital on Thursday, at my follow-up appointment.

I'm just about at my front door when the phone buzzes. It is an unlisted number. 'Hello, Nick ... '

'Jackie, so nice to hear from you. What ... ' I say, my spirits perking up immediately. But she doesn't let me finish.

'Can you come over?'

'Sure. Is something wrong?' The tone of her request is odd. Something is amiss.

'No honey, nothing is wrong. We're all good.'

Jackie is in trouble. First she's never called me 'honey' before and second, she indicated there was more than one person there. 'Okay, see you soon,' I say. I need to tackle this sensibly. Her request, normally, would have me charging down there and knocking on the door. But I suspect a trap.

After doing some preparations I find myself at the back of Jackie's duplex. She has the first-level flat, only a little higher than the ground floor flat due to the sloped land. I'd had to walk quietly down a long concrete path with a garden next to the two-storey block and a fence along the other side. I hope the door is unlocked as I expect "they", whoever "they" are, are inside. After ascending a couple of steps, I try the knob. It turns, so I push gently and tiptoe inside. I close the door, making sure the connection is soundless. I peer around the corner of the laundry. Nothing. I wander down the hall, passing the bathroom on the right and the bedrooms on the left. As I get to the living room with the kitchen on the right, I see the back of a man's head. He is sitting on the sofa but I can't see Jackie.

I sneak up and point the gun at him. 'Hands on your head and get up slowly,' I say.

He does as requested. He stays put and I walk around but instead of the unwelcome visitor being Antonovich, as I'd anticipated, it's his brother-in-law, the political candidate. I've seen Kuklev's photo on a website so I know who he is. He smiles.

'Where's Jackie?' I ask.

Magnus Kuklev is a man with ordinary features, someone who wouldn't stand out in any group of people. He is of medium height and build. He possesses bloodless lips and looks straight at me. 'What you wrote is different from your commission.'

'You don't pay me.'

'Is that the problem? You want money?'

'I write the truth. I don't tailor it to what my paymasters want,' I say, wanting to wipe the smirk off his face.

'Drop the gun,' a voice says.

I look in the direction of the comment and see a female holding a gun to a small girl's head. It's Katherine Antonovich. 'Where is Jackie?' I ask, not moving my pistol away from Kuklev.

At that moment Jackie exits a door and crashes into the woman who falls and loses the grip of her gun. But Jackie has her hands tied and she has a tape plastered across her mouth so she can't do any more. I fire a bullet into Kuklev's leg. Kuklev screams and I advance on Katherine Antonovich, who raises her hands. I pick her gun off the floor and give it to Jackie to hold between the tied wrists. 'Hold this while I untie you,' I say.

A knock on the door halts progress. I walk to the front door and let in uniformed police. I'd called them before my visit, fearing the worst. They round up Kuklev and the lovely looking but deceitful Mrs Antonovich, and I help Jackie and the ten-year-old girl into an ambulance. I stay behind with a detective and tell my story.

***

After driving up and down I finally find a parking spot near the hospital entrance. I park the car then place some coins into the meter. It annoys me that parking at hospitals is so expensive. Surely the main business is providing health services. I walk along until I find the right block then take the elevator to level seven. I ask at reception for the number of the ward in which Jackie and the young girl are recovering. The receptionist guides me around a corner to a ward that is closed when I reach it.

I enter and see the young girl lying in bed with Jackie in a chair beside her. Jackie is thumbing through a magazine. 'Hello, you two. How are you doing?'

Jackie looks up and smiles. 'Hi, come over here and give me a kiss.'

I comply while the youngster looks on. When I stand again, I say, 'You're looking better.'

'Thanks. This is my niece Amy who seems to be okay. The doctor just wants her in here for a while to see whether she's suffering from shock.'

'And you?'

'Apart from some bruises, I'm fine. I'm so glad to see you.'

'Really? You never called after your last visit to me.'

'I know but I had to return home and deal with some family matters. That's why I have Amy. My sister needed a break because of her husband's illness. I'll tell you all about it once we've been discharged.'

'How much longer will you be in here?'

'An overnight stay is all. Just to make sure Amy is okay.'

I look around. The room is clean and it has a large screen television on the wall as well as a bed for Jackie. 'The place looks cosy enough.'

'Yes, it's good. I'm sorry about the ambush. I didn't know what else to do. What made you realise I was in danger?'

'You called me honey.'

Jackie laughs. 'So you caught on. But you were nearly undone with that crazy woman who was sitting with us in the bedroom. I hope she's put away for many years.'

'Luckily your feet weren't bound,' I say. 'The police were close thank God but that mad Russian woman may still have shot me if you hadn't intervened. My call to the emergency number before I left home proved vital.'

'Who was that fellow? And why did he target us?'

'He's a politician and he's the woman's brother. Her husband was behind the original kidnapping. Now I hope they all get lengthy sentences.'

On my way home I consider what has happened to me over the space of a few weeks. Perhaps I'll write a book but it will need to be fiction so that I don't incriminate myself. We'll see.

Chapter 41 Sunday, several weeks later

It's hot. The sun bakes our sun-screened white bodies. I try to control the craft's sail to turn around so we can go back to our starting point but the thing is not behaving. The wind pushes us along the narrow stream, further towards the ocean.

Jackie looks amused as she watches me grapple with the controls of the small vessel. 'Are we stuck here forever?'

'Looks like it,' I say.

'Why don't you wave to a passing boat?'

'To be rescued?'

'Yes. Is that so implausible?'

'Embarrassing, more like,' I say.

But before more can be said, the wind gusts furiously and the boat changes course. Fifteen minutes later we are able to dock and walk back to our hotel room on the Pacific island of Vanuatu. We shower together, thoroughly washing sand and salt off each other's bodies. This process takes longer than it should as we take the opportunity to sample various areas with our mouths and tongues.

Once dressed, we're ready for a relaxing stroll and afternoon tea. After wandering round the hotel passageways, having only explored the exterior in our two-day stay, we order coffee and tea. With the trial of Kuklov and the Antonovichs scheduled soon, and as key witnesses, we'd decided to take a break.

'It's nice here. Why don't we extend our booking?' Jackie pours some tea into a cup.

I pick up my cup of cappuccino and regard her. 'Absolutely. No need to go back to a world of intrigue and corruption.'

We know we'll return but it's pleasant to daydream about living in tranquillity and peace. That's never going to happen but a change of location and activity can restore a modicum of sanity. After a couple of life-threatening experiences, a future spent in this paradise seems immensely appealing.

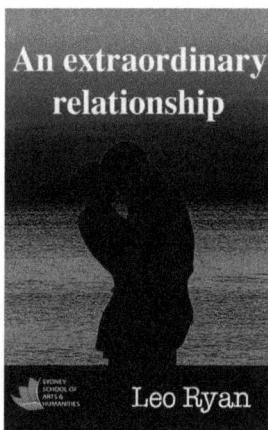

Angela's Anorexia:
The story
of my mother

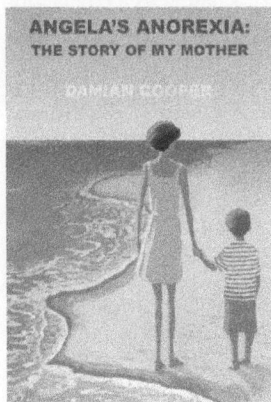

A son's story of the debilitating illness, anorexia nervosa, that his single mother suffered from throughout his childhood. The mother and son formed a close bond and the boy's description of their life together is filled with both joy and sadness. A true story showing the boy's experience of growing up fast in Australia and New Zealand, caring for his mother while coming to understand her sickness and his need to develop an independent spirit early on.

Damian Cooper has written a straightforward, honest and loving account of his boyhood, set against a poignant parallel story of his mother's excessive focus on body image, food, diet and exercise.

Category: SELF-HELP/EATING DISORDERS AND BODY IMAGE

ARCO:
the legend
of the blue vortex

An exciting new story from first-time novelist, **Ferdinando Manzo**, ARCO explores man's battle with the sea in an attempt to seek solace.

The story is set in two different eras: on the high seas among ancient pirates and in contemporary Europe ravaged by war. The legend of the blue vortex – a door into another world – is the central focus of both periods.

An adventure story, it also raises philosophical questions about love and the purpose of life.

Category: FICTION MAGICAL REALISM/ROMANCE/FANTASY

Burma My Mother
And Why I Had To Leave

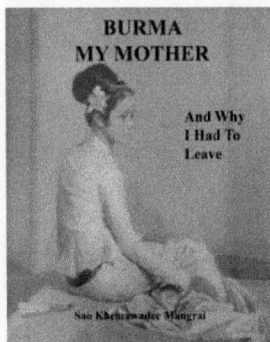

Myanmar's future is informed by its past - and BURMA MY MOTHER tells it like it is.

A valuable story of living through good times and plenty of bad in Burma, now known as Myanmar, before an escape to a new life of freedom.

Author **Sao Khemawadee Mangrai**'s husband, Hom, was imprisoned for 5 years, and his father was shot and killed sitting alongside independence leader, General Aung San, when he was assassinated.

Khemawadee grew up in a Shan state in the north-east of Myanmar, previously known as Burma, and now lives in Sydney. Her sad memories are also infused by the beauty of the country and the grace of Myanmar's Buddhist culture.

Category: MEMOIR

Drenched
by the Sun

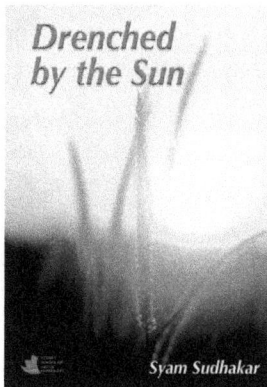

I, who prophesy
by reading the stars and the wind,
now think of that country ...

Syam Sudhakar 'has an eye for the strange
and the uncanny and a way of building
translucent metaphors,' according to leading South Indian poet, K. Satchidanandan.

An award-winning poet who writes in English
and Malayalam, Sudhakar is based in Kerala, teaching and researching Indian poetry.

Category: POEMS

Night Road to Life

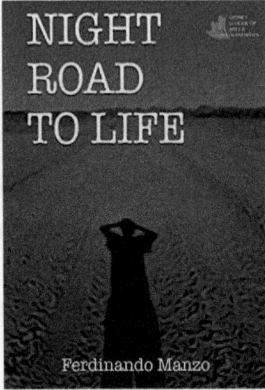

Themes of the sea and the emotions, particularly the deeply felt joys and melancholies experienced by men, are a touchstone of NIGHT ROAD TO LIFE.

Ferdinando Manzo's thoughts are not bound to fluidity; they fly to the greatest heights of exhilaration in poems such as, *The sky above us*, which displays 'a mantle of stars that burns in my heart' and in the evocative lines of *Eclipse*: 'the moon rose, bright between the eyelids of the night'. Even the constellation Andromeda is given due recognition, breaking her chains and ready for revenge, before another poem *The voice of the universe* explores 'a hidden legend as far away as waves in outer space'.

A distinctive quality of this collection of poems is its musicality – the sounds of words carefully chosen, and their rhythms. The pleasing effect of the sensuality of sounds, ranging from gentleness to the drama of sex, is in tune with the gamut of human emotion.

Category: POEMS

Reported Missing

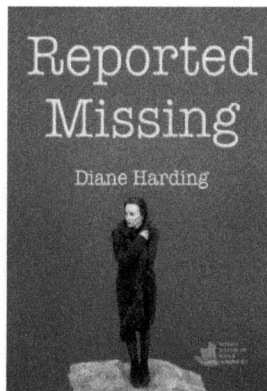

Di Harding's novel is set in a very contemporary Sydney, taking in multi-layered sights and sounds, from the northern beaches to performances at the Sydney Opera House.

The plot spans the complications of what a woman must consider if she is to save her children from domestic violence. And the main character has good reason to hold fears for her life.

What would you do if your daughter was missing and you thought your son-in-law was somehow involved? Is there someone who could help you, or would you take matters into your own hands?

She does, and so the terror begins – from vile and personal harassment to life threatening acts, until she is ready to commit murder.

Her obsession with killing grows in her mind until she begins to plan and plot. Can she actually do it? Then something shocking happens to make up her mind.

The story ends on an upbeat for a new life ahead for the family.

Category: DOMESTIC VIOLENCE
CRIME FICTION/SYDNEY NOVEL
AUSTRALIAN FICTION

Road to Mandalay Less Travelled

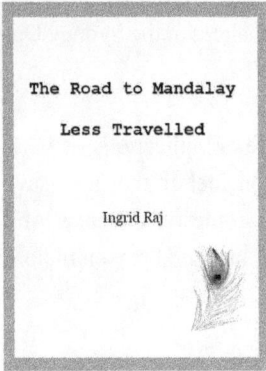

'The Road to Mandalay Less Travelled' by **Ingrid Raj** provides research on a selection of Anglo-Burmese writing published from the period of British rule in Burma up until 2007.

What Raj shares with us in this study is the knowledge she gained about the value of social resistance achieved through writing. Both fiction and non-fiction texts are included in arguing a case that these might be viewed as tools of often ambivalent resistance against oppressive regimes, both local and colonial. Her research deserves a wider readership than was initially provided, and to this aim Sydney School of Arts & Humanities presents the work as its first publication in this new category of Essays & Theses.

We hope that specialist researchers as well as members of the general reading public take this opportunity to learn more about the culture of the people of Myanmar through their unique approach to storytelling, based largely on their religious understanding, their rich store of folk legend and their chequered history.

Category: MEMOIR/LITERATURE/BURMA-HISTORY

Road to Rishi Konda

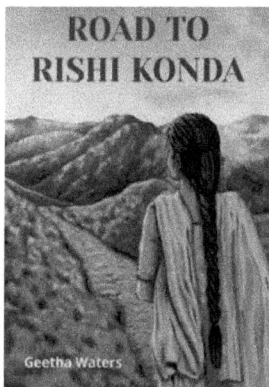

'ROAD TO RISHI KONDA' by **Geetha Waters** is a memoir of insight and charm, with a serious educational purpose. The author recalls delightful and stimulating stories from her childhood to throw light on the work of the philosopher J. Krishnamurti as a revolutionary 20th century educator.

At once fascinating and enchanting, Geetha Waters' stories centre on a girl growing up in Kerala and Andhra Pradesh in the '60s and '70s.

These youthful tales are underpinned by Geetha's deep understanding of childhood education, based both on her academic studies and in practice in her daily life as a mother and childcare professional.

Written from a child's perspective, the tales of awakening to life offer the reader an opportunity to appreciate how all children learn, as they draw on a deep well of curiosity that needs to be respected.

Category: BIOGRAPHY & AUTOBIOGRAPHY
PERSONAL MEMOIR/EDUCATORS

What's in a Name?
20 People - 20 Stories

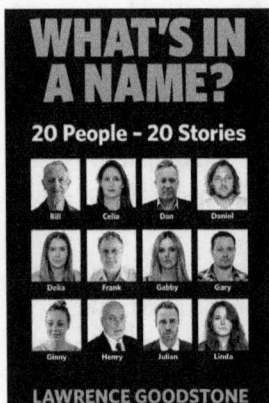

This collection of short stories will appeal to readers who are attracted to snapshots of the human condition. While set in Australia, the stories reflect universal themes. They range over a number of genres from crime to science fiction, from human weakness to human strength, and capture pockets of life with uncanny accuracy and sensitivity.

The author, Lawrence Goodstone, is a retired public servant who spent his professional life writing for others. With a background ranging from teaching to immigrant services as well as assisting in the delivery of the 2000 Olympic Games in Sydney, he is now in a position to write for himself and create stories from a life well lived.

Category: FICTION/SHORT STORY/SYDNEY STORIES
FICTION/AUSTRALIAN FICTION

Jiddu Krishnamurti World Philosopher
Revised Edition

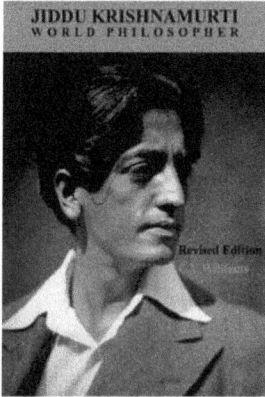

The life of the 20th-century philosopher Jiddu Krishnamurti was truly astonishing. As this new updated edition shows, people from all over the world would gather to hear him speak the wisdom of the ages.

Biographer **Christine (CV) Williams** carried out research over a period of four years to write this ebook account of Krishnamurti's life. She studied his major archive of personal correspondence and talks, and interviewed people who knew him intimately.

Krishna was born into poverty in a South Indian village, before being adopted by a wealthy English public figure, Annie Besant. As an adult he settled in California, travelling to India and England every year to give public lectures that inspired spiritual seekers beyond any single religion.

Category: BIOGRAPHY

www.ingramcontent.com/pod-product-compliance
Lightning Source LLC
Chambersburg PA
CBHW031154270326
41931CB00006B/264